Kauai

Hiking Trails

Craig Chisholm

The Fernglen Press
473 Sixth Street
Lake Oswego, Oregon 97034

Copyright © 1991
by Craig McRae Chisholm

All Rights Reserved

This book may not be reproduced in whole
or in part in any form without the prior
written permission of the author.

Maps: Courtesy of U.S. Geological Survey
Printed by Print Tek West, Salem, Oregon
Printed in the United States of America

Cover photo by Ray Atkeson

Publisher's Cataloging in Publication
(Prepared by Quality Books Inc.)

Chisholm, Craig.
    Kauai : hiking trails / Craig Chisholm. —
    p. cm.
    Includes bibliographical references and index.
    ISBN 0-9612630-3-2

    1. Hiking—Hawaii—Kauai—Guide-books.   2. Trails—Hawaii—Kauai—
Guide-books.   3. Kauai (Hawaii)—Description and travel—1981- —
Guide-books.   I. Title.

    GV199.42.H32   919.69'4044
                                               QBI91-419

Hanakapiai Falls

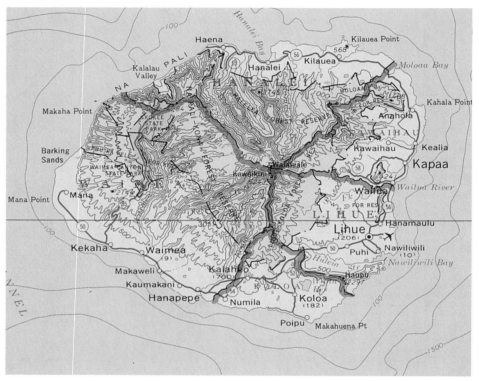

Island of Kauai

Contents

Pooman Canyon Vista

Kawaikoi Stream

View from the End of Kohua Ridge Trail

Switchbacks along Kuilau Ridge

Picnic Shelter on Kuilau Ridge Trail

The Na Pali Coast

Keahua Forestry Arboretum

Nounou Mountain — The Sleeping Giant

Polihale State Park

Helicopter Venturing among the Na Pali Cliffs

Sunset at Polihale

Dedicated to

Ray Atkeson

*Photographer Laureate
Mountaineer, and Gentleman*

Acknowledgments

Many people have helped with this book. I would like to acknowledge the assistance of the personnel of the Hawaii State Department of Land and Natural Resources who have been most generous and thoughtful in providing information and answering questions; in particular, I wish to thank Ed Petteys, George Niitani, and Galen Kawakami for their generous help and advice and for their concern for the lands entrusted to them.

I also want to thank our children for their patience and their valuable suggestions in selecting the photographs; and, especially Kari for his instruction regarding the use of the computer. Above all I wish to acknowledge the hard work of Eila, my wife, who believes not in talking, but in doing.

Craig Chisholm, Lake Oswego, Oregon

Editor:
   Eila Chisholm
Photography:
   Craig and Eila Chisholm
Cover Photo:
   Ray Atkeson, *The Na Pali Coast*
Cover Design:
   L.grafix, Portland, Oregon

Use of the Book

The trails described in this book are all accessible to the public and are administered by the State of Hawaii, either by the Division of Forestry and Wildlife or the Division of State Parks.

The first section in this book gives an introduction to the natural history of the Hawaiian Islands, with special attention to the Island of Kauai. The second section gives both general and specific information regarding hiking. Following this is a section on accommodations and making arrangements, such as, obtaining reservations and permits. A list of useful addresses is included.

The trails are organized into four different hiking areas: Kokee and Vicinity, Waimea Canyon, East Kauai, and North Kauai. The description of each area includes a topographical map of that section of the island. The trails in each of the four main hiking areas have been divided into groups in order to illustrate their proximity to each other and to clarify access to trailheads. An access map for each group of trails is included to demonstrate the location of highways, unpaved access roads, or connector trails needed to reach the trailheads.

Individual trail descriptions begin with a statistical summary. The length of time given for the hike is based on estimated total hiking time, round trip, for an average hiker. The number of calories given for each hike is what an average 150 pound hiker would burn up to complete the hike. The trails are rated as easiest, easier, harder, and hardest. Though this is designed to give some notion of the relative difficulty of the trails, these ratings are, of course, quite subjective. What is hard for one hiker many be easy for another. Each hiker must judge his or her own capabilities and not go beyond them.

Total mileage for the hike, round trip, is included in the statistical summary. If you walk the access roads to the trailheads, add the appropriate road mileage to the trail mileage. The highest and lowest elevations reached on the trail are shown to give an idea of the physical exertion required for the trail. As some trails may have many ups and downs between the highest and lowest points, the topographical map in the book should be studied to gain the best understanding of the requirements of the trail. The names of the U.S. Geological Survey maps used for the trail maps are also given in the statistical summary. The agencies within whose jurisdiction a trail lies are also named.

Each trail description includes portions of the U.S.G.S. topographical maps. These maps are at a scale of 1:24,000 (7 1/2 minutes) and have 40-foot contour intervals. The maps in the book, however, may have been enlarged or reduced. For scale, reference should be made to the mileage shown along each trail. All the maps have true north at the top. In Kauai, magnetic north lies about 11 1/2 degrees northeast of true north. Paved roads are marked by a solid line. Dirt access roads, usually 4-wheel-drive only, are marked by a double line of dashes. Trails are marked by a single line of dashes. Complete maps may be obtained by ordering, with payment in advance, from the U.S. Geological Survey, Branch of Distribution, Box 25286, Denver Federal Center, Bldg. 8i0, Denver, CO 80225, tel. (303) 236-7477. The U.S.G.S. will not take map orders over the phone, but they will give out the phone numbers of private vendors who will.

The distances, times, routes, and other facts in this book should be considered as estimates only. Descriptions of the trails can at times be subjective and, most importantly, all conditions can change. Consult the agencies within whose jurisdiction a trail lies for current and additional information. The addresses of these agencies are set out in the section on arrangements and accommodations.

The Hawaiian Islands

The Hawaiian Islands are located 2400 miles across the Pacific from San Francisco, at about the same latitude as central Mexico. The most southeasterly island in the chain is Hawaii, the "Big Island." It is 4038 square miles in area, the largest and youngest, and still growing. Lovely Maui, next along the chain, is the second largest. The smaller islands of Kahoolawe, Lanai, and Molokai are nearby and, back in geologic time, were once part of Maui. Oahu, the best known of the islands is next on the chain. On it are Honolulu, large military bases, and four-fifths of the state's population. Seventy-two miles northwest of Oahu lies Kauai, 555 square miles in area. To Kauai's southwest lies seldom-visited Niihau.

Each of the Hawaiian Islands has great natural beauty. Kauai, with its rugged terrain and Eden-like greenery is, perhaps, the loveliest of them all. Its 5,208 foot high basaltic shield volcano, Waialeale, has been deeply incised by streams, forming high cliffs and spectacular valleys. Steep topography and torrential rains have limited human habitation to the pleasant low-lying coastal areas which surround the central mountain everywhere except to the northwest, where the great Na Pali cliffs meet the sea.

The Na Pali cliffs mark the end of the mountainous, green islands. Further northwest of Kauai, in a 1500-mile line, only remnant, rocky islets and small, low, coral atolls break the surface of the vast ocean.

The Island Cycle

To better understand the Hawaiian Islands one should consider their various stages of life, for each of the islands in its time plays many parts. Kauai, now mature in its beauty, is the eldest and greenest of the mountainous islands. Its siblings to the southeast, Oahu, Molokai, Maui, Lanai, Kahoolawe, and Hawaii, are younger. To the northwest the worn islets and dry atolls are progressively older.

The origin of Kauai, according to one theory, might be traced back some tens of millions of years ago to a star passing the comet cloud lying beyond our solar system. The star's influence on the gravitational field may have nudged a comet toward our sun. Perhaps such a comet struck the central Pacific, thinning the earth's crust and leaving the hot area which has created the Hawaiian Islands. In this area, in slow succession over tens of millions of years, a multitude of volcanic mountains have risen under the depths of the Pacific, the higher ones forming the visible islands of the chain. Such islands are formed when magma issues up, layer upon layer, to build until a massive shield volcano, shaped like the gently sloping back of a turtle, rises above the sea. All the islands in the chain have been built in such a fashion. Hawaii,

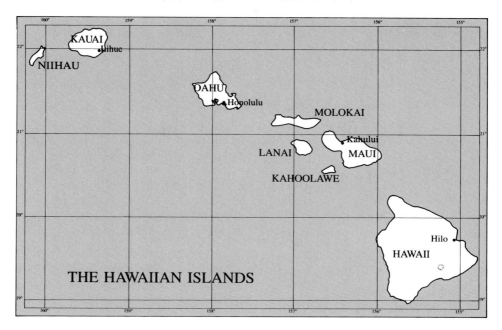

THE HAWAIIAN ISLANDS

the Big Island, is now closest to the hot area. With its active volcanoes still in this building stage it is, in the scale of geologic time, a mere mewling and puking infant compared to its older sister islands.

The islands come to life in a literal sense as soon as they rise above the sea. Algae, mosses, lichens, ferns, and forests grow on what was once sterile rock, partially protecting soils from wind and rain, though speeding chemical decomposition of the iron-rich, porous basalt. Coral fringing reefs form around the maturing islands. These living colonies of animals guard the islands against the restless waves. But while the coral holds the outer walls and grows up as the islands sink, erosion from above continues.

The islands creep northwest along with the Central Pacific plate away from the hot area. The deep vents feeding the islands' underlying magma chambers are gradually severed. As the underlying magma chambers change their chemistry, cinder cones and volcanic ash are added like a frosting to the islands. The hot area creates new islands in place of the old. The islands beyond the hot area must, as the building processes end, lose their sub-

stance to the agents of erosion: waves, rain, wind, and chemical decomposition. The great weight of the islands may cause them to subside and portions to shear off in earthquakes.

In time, today's mountainous islands will become like the dry pinnacles and coral, referred to as the Leeward Islands, stretching northwest from Kauai out to Kure Atoll. These remnants of ancient islands were once high and graced with abundant life like Kauai. Eventually the remnant islands, with their sunken basaltic foundations topped by underwater castles of coral, will slip beneath the sea as they move into waters too cold for coral to grow. They will become like the ghostly undersea mountains, once also green-clad and sunlit, lying further toward Asia. After waiting in the darkness of the ocean deep for some tens of millions of years, they will be driven into mere oblivion as part of the subduction zone ringing the Pacific.

The Island of Kauai

Kauai is now at a happy stage in its life. Its apparently extinct volcano has been sculpted to forms of exquisite beauty, but remains lofty enough to capture abundant rain from the trade winds. Though the island has subsided and its sides have been deeply stream-cut, its center is still largely intact. It consists of thick, hard, level layers of ponded lava of a massive ancient caldera, the Olokele formation. The caldera, though the largest in the Hawaiian Islands, is hard for the casual observer to discern. Young calderas, such as on the Big Island, are shaped like a pot, with the hot lava at the bottom and high sides rising around on all sides. Erosion on Kauai has long ago worn away the sides so that only the bottom of the "pot," the floor of the caldera, remains. This is the reason the top of Kauai is so nearly flat.

Kauai is just the right height to wring great quantities of moisture from the trade winds. Water from the constant heavy rains collects at the four to five thousand feet level on the flat floor of the ancient caldera in the center of the island, forming the Alakai Swamp, a rare high bog. Kauai's abundant rains nourish a thick, soil-saving garment of trees, shrubs and smaller plants covering the mountain areas and windward parts of the island. The fast growing, transplanted redwood and sugi trees of Kokee, the lush lowlands of Hanalei, and the emerald hills of the Lihue depression evidence the life-giving power of the clouds and rains. Lovely streams such as the Kawaikoi, Koaie, Hanalei, Hanakapiai, and Waimea course down the mountains. Graceful waterfalls spill into plunge pools where the cutting action of streams has been slowed by dikes and adamant layers of lava. Undercut by the action of the falls, the hard layers break off in large segments. Deep, severely cut gorges are formed. The grandest and most accessible is Waimea Canyon.

The magnificent cliffs of the Na Pali Coast, rising four thousand feet from the undercutting breakers to the top of the ancient caldera floor, are the final master-works of erosion's craft. Fringing reefs and white-sand beaches grace Kauai's shores, guarding the island, and building the future atoll.

Ecological Change

The Hawaiian Islands offered wide new opportunities to terrestrial life forms that could establish themselves. However, only at rare intervals could species successfully transit the great distances from their original homes on distant continents to reach the islands. Once a species landed, it still needed to accomplish the difficult task of establishing itself. The wind bore spores of lichens and ferns. Birds flew to the islands along with whatever stuck to their feathers or was carried in their digestive systems. Floating seeds drifted to the islands' shores.

Isolated on the islands for millions of years, the species that did establish themselves developed into new forms, diverging and filling the various ecological niches in the islands. Insects, birds, and plants all evolved until the vast majority of them became endemic (found nowhere else) to the islands. Plants such as ohia lehua established a multiplicity of forms, from tall trees to tiny bog shrubs. Snails evolved into unique sub-species on different ridges of the same island. Freed from their natural enemies, the arriving life forms lost many of their defenses. Under their new, advantageous circumstances these became unnecessary burdens. Birds became flightless. Plants lost their thorns, poisons, tough roots, and vigorous regenerative powers. This defenselessness would prove to be their undoing.

The pigs, dogs, rats, plants, diseases, and insects brought by the Polynesians a millennium and a half ago began a process of massive ecological destruction of the web of life that had evolved over millions of years of isolation. Flightless birds must have fallen easy prey to dogs and hunters. Most species were soon exterminated. Endemic plants were crowded out by introduced species. Fires caused by man soon destroyed most of the dry-land forests that once extended to the seashores of each island. Core samples from layers of alluvium in stream valleys tell the sad story.

A second wave of extinction began with Captain Cook's landing in 1778. There followed broad and continuous commerce to all parts of the world. The gentle life forms which pre-dated man and survived the influences brought by the Polynesians now faced a host of newly imported life forms: diseases, worms, insects, voracious livestock, predators, and aggressive species of plants. Vast portions of the original habitat were destroyed by wildfire and development. Whole species of endemic and indigenous plants, and the animals which depended upon them, became extinct — a complete and irretrievable evil.

The cattle, goats, sheep, horses, and large European pigs introduced by early sailing ships, ranged into wetter areas and stripped the land of vegetation, laying it open to erosion and invasive weeds. Domestic and wild livestock were steadily destroying the forested areas on all the islands until the early part of this century. When the water supplies needed by the sugar industry became imperiled, forest areas were set aside for protection and the wild cattle were destroyed. Sugar plantation interests and government agencies began to plant previously wasted areas with introduced species of trees: Norfolk Island pine, ironwood, eucalyptus, sugi, redwood, and many others.

Some of the trails described in this book lead through such plantings, now grown into large forests. Other trails lead to wondrous places which are difficult to reach and, therefore, still have most of their original plants and animals. Unfortunately, even in such places, the agents of extinction are a threat. The conservation efforts of governmental agen-cies, enlightened private landowners, and organizations such as The Nature Conservancy give a basis for hope. With proper management much can be done to preserve and even restore Hawaii's unique and rich natural legacy.

Climate and Topography

The weather in the Hawaiian Islands varies dramatically from one area to the next but is remarkably stable the year-round in any one place. The vastness of the Pacific Ocean, moderating the temperature of the trade winds blowing steadily from the northeast, minimizes seasonal change. Winter is somewhat wetter and a few degrees cooler than summer, but is usually still balmy. It may rain any time of the year. The trade winds, strongest in summer, passing over the rugged terrain, create distinct, almost invariable lines between microclimates. As the trade winds rise over the high mountainous islands, they cool to form clouds which release their moisture, more heavily on the north and northeast of each island and at higher elevations. The warm, humid Kona winds may occasionally vary the direction of the weather, bringing extremely heavy rains from the south, usually in winter.

On Kauai, the hiking trails in the Kokee area are at almost 4000 feet in elevation. Therefore, temperatures tend to be about 10-15 degrees Fahrenheit cooler than at sea level. Kokee receives approximately 60 inches of rain a year, with the driest months between June and October. The rainfall rapidly becomes heavier as one approaches the Alakai Swamp. The trails in Waimea Canyon are noticeably warmer and drier than those on the rim, though the streams on the canyon floor often flood because of rain in the mountains. The southwest side of the island, in the rain shadow of Mount Waialeale, is usually quite arid. Polihale State Park, located in the rain shadow, can be a welcome refuge during rainy weather, though hiking is limited to strolls down the beach.

Since the trails in East Kauai are fairly close to sea level, hikers nearly always enjoy balmy weather. The trails inland, near Keahua Forestry Arboretum, tend to be wetter. In North Kauai the Hanalei region receives close to 100 inches of rain a year. The beginning part of the Kalalau Trail receives more rain than areas farther along the coast. Kalalau Beach, at the end of the trail can be quite dry.

Hiking on Kauai

Equipment and Clothing

Relatively little equipment is needed for hiking on Kauai. However, temperatures drop about 3 degrees Fahrenheit for every 1,000 feet gained in elevation. Hikes into the high country around Kokee can occasionally be unpleasant and even dangerous, if the wind-swept traveler becomes wet or is overtaken by darkness. At such higher elevations waterproof and wool clothing can be useful, the latter because it retains some warmth even when wet.

At sea level, shorts and lightweight clothing are usually adequate and pleasant. Rain gear near sea level is optional; some prefer to hike in light clothing, get wet in the warm rain, and dry out later. After all, one can get only so wet. Over rough terrain stout, broken-in boots are best. However, when wet, boots are heavy and, in the damp areas of Kauai, slow to dry. Tennis shoes are fine for short hikes. However, many trails can be quite slippery, if wet, and thus lug soles may be helpful. Long pants guard against both heavy brush and sunburn. Near the sea a light hat with a brim and sunglasses are especially useful. Many visitors from less sunny regions are likely to receive painful sunburns and therefore should wear protective clothing or use sunblock (which still does not stop all harmful frequencies of light).

Tents are generally required for camping in campgrounds. They can be of value in keeping out ants and other crawly pests, particularly, at lower elevations. Plastic ground covers can double as ponchos and picnic cloths. Insect repellent, water bottles, first aid kit, matches for emergencies, extra food, whistle, knife, compass, maps, flashlights, and the usual emergency and first aid gear should be carried. Light sleeping bags of the newer synthetic materials which hold heat even if wet are best. A flashlight is especially important on late afternoon hikes. Night descends rapidly because of the low latitude. This can come as a disturbing surprise to some visiting hikers from regions farther from the equator. On the longest day of the year, June 21, sunrise is about 4:50 a.m. and sunset about 7:40 p.m. On the shortest day, December 21, sunrise is about 7:20 a.m. and sunset is about 4:55 p.m. Allow ample time in order to reach your destination before nightfall.

Precautions

Many of the trails go through areas covered by dense vegetation or are in areas with extremely rugged terrain. Know where you came from at all times. If a trail dwindles away, it is probably a false one, such as a dead-ending hunters' route or a pig trail. Retrace your steps until you are sure you are on the main trail, then look for the turnoff you missed. The cliffs and thick vegetation make cross-country travel difficult and unwise. Besides, cliffs in Hawaii are not suitable for rock climbing. The volcanic rock is universally rotten and treacherous portable handholds abound. If stranded, it is usually best to wait for daylight and try to attract help from the pesky sightseeing helicopters that fly over many areas. Vegetation may crowd in and hide drop-offs. STAY ON THE TRAIL. If you wander off the trail, over-optimistic hunters may mistake you for game, to their disappointment and your misfortune. It is a good idea to find out if hunting is going on in an area and proceed accordingly.

Hike in company; a minor sickness or injury can become a major problem if no friend can walk out to bring help. Leave your plans with a responsible person. Obtain appropriate permits and sign in at trailhead sign-in stands. Carry water, for streams may be contaminated by upstream animals or ignorant humans. If water is used from streams or rivers it is safest to treat it. Leptospirosis is found in water on the island and could be transmitted through cuts or ingestion.

Rain, even far upstream, may make stream fords impassable or cause dangerous flash floods. Wait philosophically for waters to recede, which usually takes only a few hours of patience. Beware of falling rocks in waterfalls, alongside cliffs, and under arches.

Poison oak and poison ivy are not found on the Hawaiian Islands; however, some persons are allergic to the mango tree and its fruit. The bark of the paper bark tree is highly irritating when wet and should not be used as toilet paper. Some plants can be poisonous if eaten, used for cooking skewers, or rubbed into skin. Unless you know the fruits and berries, it is best not to eat them.

A pleasant part of hiking in Kauai is that there are relatively few problems from animals. There are no poisonous snakes on Kauai. Wild pigs, though shy, might attack if harmed. Mosquitoes can be a nuisance, though they are not as suicidally ferocious as some mainland varieties. They are comparative newcomers to the Hawaiian Islands. Relatively few species are present and no species has yet established itself at elevations above about 3000 feet. All species tend to avoid strong sunlight and windy areas. Flies can be a nuisance in some areas. A few other insect pests, spiders, centipedes and scorpions, may be found, but they are usually not very troublesome.

"Rogue" waves, a combination of the amplitudes of two or more waves and much larger than the usual, may occasionally sweep the unwary into the sea. Hikers following the seacoast should not be lulled into thinking that all waves are the same size. Tidal waves hit the beaches at rare intervals. Sharks in the waters off the beaches are not noted for being man-eaters; however, some may be unaware of this general rule. Waves and currents are a far greater danger.

Crime and violence exist in Hawaii as elsewhere, though statistics indicate that the crime rate is lower than the average for the United States and Kauai has less crime than the more populous islands. Nonetheless, the same precautions should be followed as on the mainland. Just because Kauai is a paradise, hikers and especially campers, particularly adjacent to roads and populous areas, should not think themselves immune from theft and other crimes. Just as on the mainland, women should not camp and travel alone. Violent crime is unusual, but occasionally there are thefts, especially in areas frequented by tourists. Valuables should not be left unattended in tents or locked in cars. Vehicles are sometimes broken into or damaged. Marijuana patches are usually carefully hidden from the authorities and anyone else. They are highly unlikely to be found along well-traveled trails. They must be strictly avoided since they may be jealously and dangerously guarded. This is yet another reason to stay on the known trails. As a practical matter, the hazards of driving and sunburn are far greater than the hazards of crime.

Fires

Open fires are not permitted in the back country at all. Even at campsites next to paved roads open fires are prohibited except at a few designated fireplaces. This is for good reason; the fire danger is simply too great. In any case campfires in the warm lowland climate add little comfort. Firewood is scarce or damp at higher, cooler elevations.

Caution regarding fires cannot be stressed enough. Rain forest conditions give a false sense of security. Sunny skies and steady winds can dry up a rain-soaked morning forest and, through someone's carelessness, turn it into a blazing inferno by mid-afternoon. Heavy underbrush, steep slopes, high winds, and peat soils make fires extremely difficult to control. Dry humus and accumulated material on the ground is often so deep that a fire can start, burn through a wet top layer, and progress underground to burst out later and devastate large areas. Smoke in the back country may be reported as a sign of an emergency by helicopter pilots. This can be much to the embarrassment and financial cost of those who build fires in disregard of the law.

If a gas stove is to be used, purchase stove fuel or gas canisters locally, since airlines have sensibly forbidden their presence on planes. The most practical course in the back country is to travel light and dispense with the nuisance of fire making and cooking altogether.

Caring for Nature

The usual admonitions regarding minimal impact camping and hiking apply in Hawaii: pack out what you bring in, damage nothing, and bury human wastes away from water. In short, leave nature as you found it. Special emphasis must be made regarding the extreme danger of fires. Also, cleaning your shoes and equipment before you leave one area for another, especially to another island, should not be neglected. Unless you do so, you may become the unwitting carrier of noxious introduced seeds into areas formerly unspoiled. Avoid trenching around tents.

On a distinctly limited budget the Division of Forestry and Wildlife and the Division of State Parks take care of the trails, shelters, plants, and animals of the back country. The brushing, marking, fire fighting, cleaning, repairing, and the control of noxious introduced plants seen along the trails are their work. The personnel of these departments are keenly aware of all that needs to be protected and are remarkably dedicated to the task. It is an unfortunate fact, however, that a major part of their efforts must be diverted to merely repairing damage done by vandals and cleaning up litter. Whatever hikers can do to assist in preventing litter, fire and vandalism is of considerable benefit to the environment since it will free up resources for the critical tasks of protecting nature in Hawaii.

Arrangements and Accommodations

10 x 13" postage
1.01 recreation map

Most trails described in this book do not require permits for day hiking since they are on lands under the jurisdiction of the Division of Forestry and Wildlife or the Division of State Parks. However, permits are required beyond Hanakapiai Beach on the Na Pali Coast. These may be obtained at the Division of State Parks.

Permits for camping are always required. These may be obtained from the governmental agencies whose addresses are given below. It is a good idea to do this well in advance to be assured of reservations, especially at campgrounds next to roads. The camps in Kokee State Park and Waimea Canyon are in most demand in late summer during the trout season. Cabins and bunkhouses usually require reservations. There are time limits for stays. Various fees and regulations apply. Some reservations must be obtained well in advance.

The governmental agencies as well as the private sources listed below will provide current information and literature concerning hiking, camping, and related subjects.

Addresses for Reservations and Permits

Department of Land and Natural Resources
Division of Forestry and Wildlife
P.O. Box 1671
3060 Eiwa Street, Room 306
Lihue, Kauai, HI 96766
(808) 241-3433

Department of Land and Natural Resources
Division of State Parks
P.O. Box 1671
3060 Eiwa Street, Room 306
Lihue, Kauai, HI 96766
(808) 241-3444 *4445*

Department of Public Works
Parks and Recreation, County of Kauai
4396 Rice Street
Lihue, Kauai, HI 96766
(808) 245-8821

Kokee Lodge
P.O. Box 819
Waimea, Kauai, HI 96796
(808) 335-6061

Camp Sloggett (YWCA)
3094 Elua
Lihue, Kauai, HI 96766
(808) 245-5959

Kahili Mountain Park
P.O. Box 298
Koloa, Kauai, HI 96756
(808) 742-9921

Camp Naue (YMCA)
P.O. Box 1786
Lihue Kauai, HI 96766
(808) 246-9090

Bed and Breakfast Hawaii
P.O. Box 449
Kapaa, Kauai, HI 96746
(808) 742-6995

Kay Barker's Bed and Breakfast
P.O. Box 740
Kapaa, Kauai, Hawaii 96746

U.S. Geological Survey
Branch of Distribution
Box 25286
Denver Federal Center, Bldg. 8i0
Denver, CO 80225
(303) 236-7477

Campsites, Cabins, and Bunkhouses

Campsites in State Parks and Forest Reserve areas are improved to various degrees by the Division of State Parks or the Division of Forestry and Wildlife. Some are near roads, which can be paved, rock, or 4-wheel-drive dirt (undriveable when wet) roads. The simple roof shelters usually associated with the Division of State Parks and Division of Forestry and Wildlife campsites can be used to keep out of sun and rain. They are mentioned in the trail description when located along the trails. In the back country water must be packed in, as any available surface water should be treated. No fires are allowed in the back country, only backpacking stoves.

Most camping areas usable in connection with trails are in Kokee State Park and Waimea Canyon. There are no campsites along the trails in the East Kauai area or in the Hanalei Valley. The Kalalau Trail on the Na Pali Coast has three wilderness camping areas.

Cabins and bunkhouses are located at Kokee (Kokee Lodge and Camp Sloggett), in the south near Koloa (Kalihi Mountain Park) and on the north coast at

Haena (YMCA Camp Naue).

The better cabins and camping areas and their locations, starting from Kokee State Park and going around the island to the Na Pali Coast, are described below. Addresses for reservations or information are listed above.

Kokee Lodge, a well-run, private concession, is located in the highlands of Kokee State Park next to the Park Headquarters. Its moderately priced cabins, including kitchens and fireplaces, can be most welcome after a day of hiking in the lush, wet areas at the top of the island.

Camp Sloggett (YWCA), half a mile down Kumuwela Road from Kokee State Park Headquarters, has a bunkhouse and lodge accommodations close to Kokee's trails.

Kokee State Park has tent sites, showers, toilets, picnic tables, and a pavilion on a quiet hillside at the east end of the grassy field at the center of the park. For permits and information contact the Division of State Parks.

The Division of Forestry and Wildlife has primitive forest camps for tent camping along the 4-wheel-drive Mohihi (Camp 10) Road at Kawaikoi Camp and Sugi Grove. This dirt road starts near Kokee State Park Headquarters and leads east, toward the Alakai Swamp. See map and trail descriptions in the Mohihi (Camp 10) Road Access section. For permits and information contact the Division of Forestry and Wildlife.

Waimea Canyon has several primitive forest camps, with simple roof shelters, along the trails on the canyon floor. These are far from paved roads. Wiliwili Camp is next to the Waimea River at the junction of the Kukui and Waimea Trails. Poachers' Camp is half a mile downstream from Wiliwili Camp and then a quarter mile up Waialae Stream, which comes in from the east. It is the least desireable since it is fairly close to a 4-wheel-drive road. Kaluahaula Camp is up the Waimea River about half a mile from Wiliwili Camp, on the east bank. Hipalau Camp is about a mile up from where Koaie Stream joins the Waimea River. Lonomea Camp is another mile and three-quarters upstream from Hipalau Camp. See map and description in the Waimea Canyon access section. For permits and information contact the Division of Forestry and Wildlife.

Polihale State Park is in the dry, flat area at the extreme west side of Kauai, beyond Kekaha and the Navy's Barking Sands Pacific Missile Range Facility (with a small Navy Exchange). The isolated beach offers limited walks and wonderful sunsets with the islands of Niihua and Lehua in the distance to the southwest. The unpaved road to it can be impassable to vehicles in wet weather. Grills, tables, pavilions, toilets, and showers are available. The park can be used in conjunction with hiking in the often wet Kokee area, about a 45-minute drive away. For permits and information contact the Division of State Parks.

Kahili Mountain Park is owned and operated by the Seventh Day Adventist Church. Its cabins and cabinettes are in a natural setting, centrally located near Koloa, 20 minutes east from Lihue airport and 7 miles north from Poipu.

Camp Naue (YMCA), in Haena, less than two miles from the start of the Kalalau Trail on the North Coast of Kauai, has bunkhouses and a tent-camping area.

The Na Pali Coast has three camping areas located along the Kalalau Trail: Hanakapiai Beach (two miles in), Hanakoa (six miles in), and Kalalau Beach (11 miles in). These are administered by the Division of State Parks and require permits for their use, as does hiking beyond Hanakapiai Beach. The camping areas are described with the Hanakapiai, Hanakoa, and Kalalau Trails. All are primitive sites. For permits and information contact the Division of State Parks.

County beach campgrounds, under the jurisdiction of the Kauai Department of Public Works, Parks and Recreation, are located close to the Highways which follow the coast all the way from Waimea to Haena. They are far removed from hiking areas and are in relatively populated areas with all the associated disadvantages and potential problems relating to public order. These campgrounds are: Lucy Wright (near Waimea), Salt Pond (near Hanapepe), Niumalu (near Nawiliwili), Hanamaulu (near Lihue), Anini (near Kilauea), Hanalei (near Hanalei), and Haena (near Haena). Though providing beach access, these campgrounds are generally not preferred for visitors. For permits and current information contact Department of Parks and Recreation.

Conventional Lodging

The hotels and condominiums on Kauai are located almost entirely on the eastern half of the island, from Princeville in the north to Poipu in the south. Simple economy motels can be found in Lihue for those on modest budgets. Since the airport is in Lihue, these motels sometimes can be nicely used by visitors on the day of arrival or departure.

There are a number of bed and breakfast organizations, the largest being Bed and Breakfast Hawaii, P.O. Box 449, Kapaa, Kauai, HI 96746, (808) 742-6995. Kay Barker's Bed and Breakfast is located on the west side of Nounou Mountain (the "Sleeping Giant"), P.O. Box 740, Kapaa, Kauai, HI 96746.

Guides such as *Kauai: A Paradise Guide*, *Fodor's Hawaii*, *Hidden Hawaii*, and *Birnbaum's Hawaii* have details, current phone numbers, and prices concerning lodging.

Transportation

Reduced fares may be available on inter-island jet flights for military, standbys, youths, off-hour fliers, holders of commuter tickets, and passengers with tickets purchased in connection with flights from outside the state. Check with your travel agent. Bus transportation is, at present, unavailable on Kauai. Hitchhiking can be dangerous because of the narrow shoulders on roads. Rental cars are available with widely varying rates. Car rental clerks, observing camping gear, occasionally refuse to rent to campers without proof of reservations at a hotel. Car rental contracts for passenger cars may contain clauses prohibiting use of cars off paved roads and voiding insurance where so used. Occasionally, cars left at trailheads have been broken into. As in most places in Hawaii, the trails are generally too steep, rough, and root-covered for mountain bikes.

Kawaikoi Stream

Kokee and Vicinity

A map of the mountainous northwest corner of Kauai will show the high country of Kokee State Park and the adjacent Forest Reserves seemingly close to the Na Pali Coast on the north and Waimea Canyon to the south. To a hiker on the ground it is all much different. The hidden valleys and warm beaches of the Na Pali Coast, tantalizingly in view below, cannot be reached from the high country on foot. To reach the Na Pali Coast one must drive all the way around the island. Likewise, from the forested upland trails that wind through Kokee State Park one may survey the great cliffs and deep chasms of Waimea Canyon. However, only the Kukui Trail provides direct access to the canyon floor, two to three thousand feet below.

Kauai's high country was formed by the floor of an ancient caldera in Kauai's long extinct shield volcano and by the one portion of the volcano's sloping side which remains largely intact. The level floor of the ancient caldera was repeatedly covered with ponds of lava. The sides of the caldera, which once rose as cliffs ringing the ponded lavas, have long since been eroded away, which explains the relative flatness of the high country in the Kokee area. The caldera floor is now covered by thick forests and the Alakai Swamp. Erosion also cut into the softer, sloping sides of the shield volcano which once surrounded the caldera. Now, high,

impassable cliffs drop off from the floor of the old caldera virtually encircling it, except on its lee side. The lee side of Kauai, where Kokee and Waimea Canyon are located, has been sheltered for millions of years from the heaviest of the rains brought by the northeast trade winds. Thus, this side is the least eroded. The still intact slope of the volcano makes a ramp upon which the roads providing access up to the high country have been built.

Kokee State Park is located in Kauai's cool and somewhat wet high country. Its built-up area includes a broad grassy lawn, apparently owned by the moa, a type of jungle fowl, which march across it. Surrounding the lawn are the Kokee Campground, Kokee Natural History Museum and gift shop, and well-managed Kokee Lodge, which includes rental cabins, a restaurant and a gift shop, and Kokee State Park Headquarters, which is a small ranger cabin. Kokee State Park's hillside campground, though often wet, is adequate and has fire pits and showers. The museum is well worth visiting before hiking and will give a good orientation to the geography and natural history of the area. Camp Sloggett (YWCA) is about half a mile away, down Kumuwela Road.

Kokee Lodge's restaurant serves breakfast, lunch and, on weekends, dinner. The food is good and the restaurant and gift shop have a certain charm to them. It is

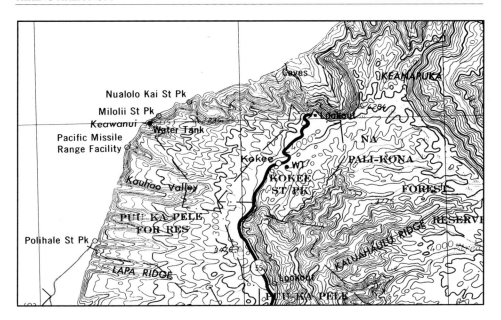

particularly pleasant to stay at Kokee Lodge's rustic cabins in connection with hiking the trails in the area. A pleasant hike, a good meal at the restaurant, and an evening by the fire in one of the cabins are a combination much appreciated and rarely found elsewhere.

The trails in Kokee and its vicinity are divided into three trail groupings according to their proximity and access. In the first group are those trails which have trailheads on paved Highway 550. These day-hikes may be easily reached by passenger car in any weather. They can be hiked nicely in combination with stays in the Kokee area or elsewhere on the island.

The second group of trails have trailheads starting on the 4-wheel-drive Halemanu or Kumuwela Roads. The trailheads are not far down these dirt roads from Kokee State Park Campground, Kokee Lodge, and Camp Sloggett. It is not necessary to use a car to hike these trails, since the dirt roads can be walked as part of the hikes.

The third group includes the trails that are far down the 4-wheel-drive Mohihi (Camp 10) Road, with trailheads at least more than three miles from Park Headquarters. This dirt road can become undriveable when wet, especially on its further reaches. Fortunately, Kawaikoi and Sugi Grove Campsites are situated about four miles down the road. The campsites can be hiked to and then used as base camps for hiking the trails in this area, if vehicular transportation is not an alternative.

Highway 550

All the trailheads for the trails in this section are on paved Highway 550. They can be easily reached by passenger car even when the dirt roads to the other trails in the area are wet and difficult to travel. The trails can be hiked nicely in combination with stays at Kokee State Park Campground, Kokee Lodge, and Camp Sloggett (YWCA). They can also be hiked completely or in part by those driving up for the day from other parts of the island.

The Nualolo and Awaawapuhi Trails, which are day-hikes, start close to the built-up area of Kokee State Park. Both lead down through native forest, now rare, to the high cliffs over-looking the Na Pali Coast. The trails are connected toward their lower ends by the Nualolo Cliff Trail and, therefore, all three can be combined to make a nine and a half mile loop trip. The Awaawapuhi Trail offers the better views, has twin metal-railed lookouts at its end, and is well-maintained. Endemic plants along the trail have been labelled. The Nualolo Trail has some spots which are steep and slippery when wet and, in its final segment, with the best views, it is quite exposed to cliffs. That segment can be skipped by taking the Nualolo Cliff Trail, which offers just as good views, but may be hard to follow if it has not been recently brushed. The climate tends to be drier toward the end of these trails than at the top. They are best hiked early in the

Kalalau Valley

morning in order to allow plenty of time to return uphill before night's rapid descent.

The Kaluapuhi Trail, sometimes called the Plum Grove Trail, was once a favorite trail for picking South African plums in early summer. The plum trees have been crowded out in recent years and have little left to offer. Blackberries infest the

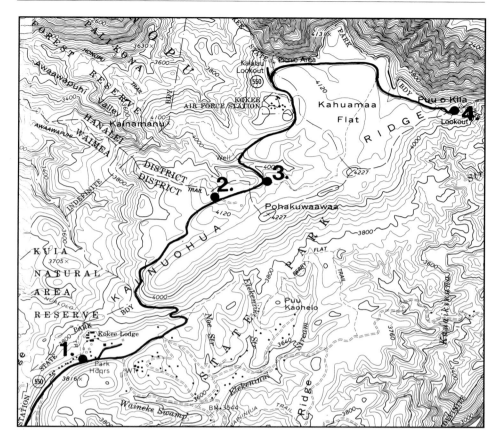

area and are getting worse. The best aspect of the trail is that it provides a forest trail, instead of a walk up the narrow highway, for those wishing to reach the Kalalau Lookout on foot. The Kalalau Lookout is definitely a place not to miss since it offers, perhaps, the most impressive view in all the Hawaiian Islands.

The Pihea Trail is at the end of Highway 550, in the Na Pali-Kona Forest Reserve. For the first mile the trail follows easily along the rim of the Kalalau Valley, offering excellent photography. It becomes more difficult and muddy as it turns downhill and passes through the fringes of the Alakai Swamp. The trail crosses the Alakai Swamp Trail and ends at Kawaikoi Camp on Mohihi (Camp 10) Road. The Pihea Trail can be used as an alternate access to the Alakai Swamp Trail, if Mohihi (Camp 10) Road is undriveable.

1. Nualolo

Highway 550
2 hours down, 3 hours up
1100 calories; hardest
7.5 miles, round trip
Highest point: 3800 feet
Lowest point: 2234 feet
Map: Makaha Point
Division of Forestry and Wildlife

A quiet walk through a mostly endemic Hawaiian forest and broad views of the open, wind-swept areas above the cliffs along the Na Pali Coast are the rewards for the substantial effort required on this trail. The upper portions of the trail pass through the Kuia Natural Area Reserve before the trees thin out as the trail reaches drier, more open areas in the Na Pali-Kona Forest Reserve closer to the tops of the steep cliffs of the Na Pali Coast. In places the trail is steep, deeply rutted, or dangerously exposed. It may be muddy and slippery, especially in some of the steeper areas.

Route: The Nualolo Trail begins on Highway 550, just below Kokee State Park Headquarters. It starts up sharply for about 400 yards and then leads generally downhill and northwesterly through dense forest and over occasional grassy areas. A little over 1.5 miles from its start the trail curves to the left. At about this point, an old, now abandoned, trail once continued to the north and is still shown on topographical maps. The official trail leads generally westward and downhill through drier and drier forest. At about the 3-mile mark the trail splits. Follow the right fork, which leads down a steep incline before the Nualolo Cliff Trail comes in from the right at about 3.2 miles. The trail then continues generally downhill through open country onto the bench land on the south rim of the

Nualolo Valley

Nualolo Valley. It follows the rim until it officially ends at a U.S.G.S. survey marker titled "Lolo No. 2."

It is dangerous to approach the cliff edge too closely. Small rocks on eroded surfaces, which may act like ball bearings, make exceptionally treacherous footing. The final section of the Nualolo Trail can be omitted and a portion of Nualolo Cliff Trail taken instead to see

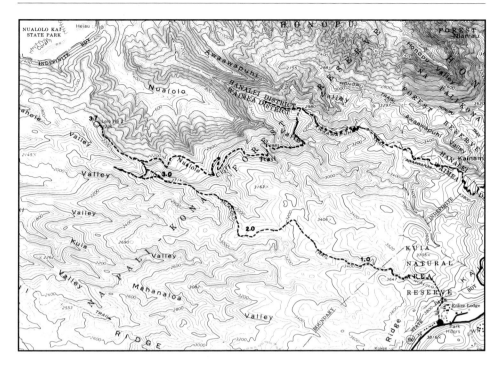

good views of the Nualolo Valley. Check with the Park Headquarters for current information regarding trail conditions and hunting in the area. Take flashlights since night falls quickly and the return will take longer than the downhill leg. The trails are for day use only. Fire danger can be extreme.

Nualolo Cliff Trail is a connector trail between the Nualolo and the Awaawapuhi Trails. Its ends are located about three miles from the Awaawapuhi Trail's trail-head and about 3.2 miles from the beginning of the Nualolo Trail. The trail follows a scenic winding two-mile course above the Nualolo Valley, passing a Division of Forestry and Wildlife picnic area. If all three trails are hiked together they compose a nine and a half-mile loop which includes the 1.6 mile distance between the two trailheads along Highway 550.

2. Awaawapuhi
Highway 550
1½ hours down, 2¼ hours up
1000 calories; harder
6.5 miles, round trip
Highest point: 4100 feet
Lowest point: 2560 feet
Maps: Haena, Makaha Point
Division of Forestry and Wildlife

Awesome views of the Na Pali Coast and its isolated, hanging valleys make this trail one of the best for photography in Hawaii. The trail descends 1500 feet through native dryland forests to twin viewpoints above the sheer cliffs dropping into the remote Awaawapuhi and Nualolo Valleys. The floors of these rarely visited valleys are accessible only by water and then only after difficult climbing from the sea. However, the viewpoints provide good vantage points of the valleys and the great fluted walls enclosing them. The sight is memorable, especially, if you sit at the viewpoints and watch the sunlight and shadows play on the cliffs and sea near dawn. Every morning helicopters flutter like dragonflies in and out of the steep-cliffed valleys below. The Division of Forestry and Wildlife has marked many endemic plants along the route and has published an interpretive guide to them available at the Division's office in Lihue or at the Kokee Museum.

Fluted Cliffs

Route: From Kokee State Park Headquarters go 1.6 miles up Highway 550 toward the Kalalau Lookout. The trailhead is on the left, in the Na Pali-Kona Forest Reserve, across from a dirt road and just before the 17-mile mark on the Highway. At first the broad trail leads north and goes up a little. It then descends switchbacks, generally in a northwesterly direction. Along the way there are many numbered and labelled endemic bushes and trees. At approximately 3 miles from the start, the Nualolo Cliff Trail, which is a connector from the Nualolo Trail, leads in from the left (south). Soon after this junction, the Awaawapuhi Trail ends at the metal-railed viewpoints overlooking the sea, great cliffs, white-trailed tropic birds, and the inevitable 8 a.m. helicopters. Do not go close to the rims of the canyons. The small stones covering the hard surfaces on the eroded areas, like ball bearings on

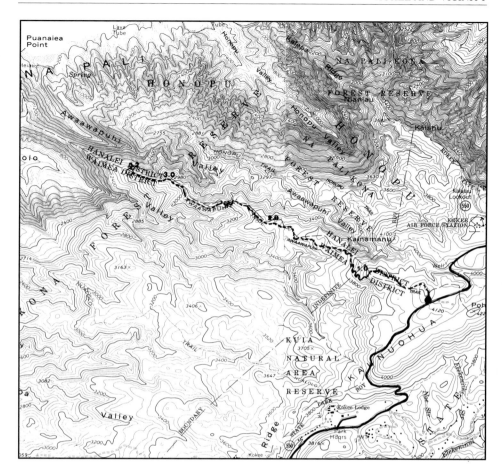

concrete, provide treacherous footing. The drop to the valley floor on either side is between 1500 and 2000 feet, depending on the bounce.

The plants in the native dryland forest are rare and the danger of fires extreme; thus, neither overnight camping nor fires are permitted. Water is unavailable.

Helicopter Venturing among the Na Pali Cliffs

3. Kaluapuhi (Plum Grove)
Highway 550
1½ hours, round trip
300 calories; easier
2 miles, round trip
Highest point: 4150 feet
Lowest point: 4030 feet
Map: Haena
Division of State Parks

This trail provides a fairly level route through a native forest being overwhelmed by introduced species of plants. The tasty South African plums which once were plentiful along the trail in the early summer are now mostly gone. The 4000-foot elevation of the trail put the plums safely above the main range of the introduced Mediterranean fruit fly, which attacks nearly all fruits. Nonetheless, fruit trees need human care to allow them to compete successfully against other species. Without it the plum trees in this area have gradually been crowded out by other plants. There are no distant views from this trail itself, but from the end of the trail along Highway 550 it is only 0.3 miles to the Kalalau Valley Lookout with its grand vista of the Kalalau Valley.

Route: The trailhead is 1.9 miles north (uphill) from Kokee State Park Headquarters on the right along Highway 550. The trail goes generally east through native ohia forest which is fast becoming overgrown with introduced grasses, blackberries, and guava. At 0.4 miles the trail splits, with the right branch initially heading southeast to gradually disappear into the undergrowth in less than half a mile. The left branch heads north to reach Highway 550 at 1.0 miles from the beginning of the trail and 0.3 miles east of the Kalalau Lookout.

The trail passes through heavy stands of introduced grasses, a source of

Rank Vegetation along the Kaluapuhi Trail

extreme misery to hay fever sufferers. The stands sometimes reach 7 feet high, but curiously stop at the trail margins. The grasses grow readily on the disturbed laterite soil along the trail, but are unable to compete in the undisturbed forest duff.

Blackberries, a newcomer from the 1930's, thrive in spots opened to sunlight when native trees were felled by the winds of Hurricane Iwa in 1982. If the young trees could grow, they might slowly shade out the blackberries and restore

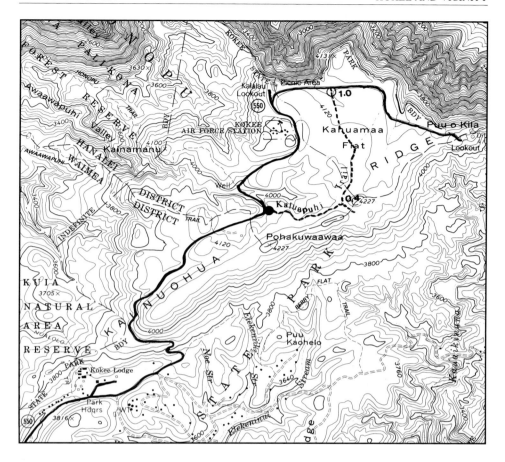

the forest. The blackberries kill them
before they get the chance. Blackberries
grow over the young trees, not only shad-
ing them, but also grasping them with
vines and sawtooth-like prickles. The
vines, given time, pull over the tops of
the young trees and saw at their tender
bark as the wind rocks the vegetation.
What ground blackberries seize, they
hold.

4. Pihea

Highway 550
2½ hours in, 3 hours out
1100 calories; harder
7.5 miles, round trip
Highest point: 4284 feet
Lowest point: 3420 feet
Map: Haena
Division of Forestry and Wildlife

Following the tops of the great fluted cliffs above the Kalalau Valley, passing through deep ohia forest and ending at peaceful Kawaikoi Camp on Mohihi (Camp 10) Road near the lovely Kawaikoi Stream, the Pihea Trail offers a wide variety of scenery. It borders the expanse of the Alakai Swamp and provides all-weather trail access to the Alakai Swamp Trail. The Pihea Trail is most pleasant early in the morning, when there is a good chance of seeing endemic Hawaiian birds feeding in the trees along the trail. Goats, descendants of the barnyard variety brought to the area by sailors in the eighteenth century, clamber with remarkable aplomb on the cliffs below. They nonchalantly take their breakfasts, sometimes on the last of some endangered species.

The ocean and sky provide an immense backdrop of varying shades of blue and white. The light plays on the fluted cliffs. Ferns, mosses, white lichen, and ohia lehua trees, with their brilliant red flowers, delight the eye.

Route: From Kokee State Park Headquarters drive up Highway 550 for 3.8 miles all the way to its end at Puu O Kila Lookout. The trail begins at the lookout and leads into the Na Pali-Kona Forest Reserve, following the remnants of an ill-considered road building attempt along the edge of the cliffs above the Kalalau Valley. As the trail approaches the Alakai

Pali above Kalalau Valley

Swamp, the vegetation becomes more luxuriant.

After 1.1 miles a steep spur leads up a short distance to the Pihea viewpoint. The main trail passes by the turnoff to the spur and becomes more difficult as it descends southerly, skirting the bogs of the Alakai Swamp. The trail becomes quite muddy and hikers should expect to get their shoes wet. At about 1.7 miles the trail crosses the Alakai Swamp Trail in a flat, swampy area crowded with small

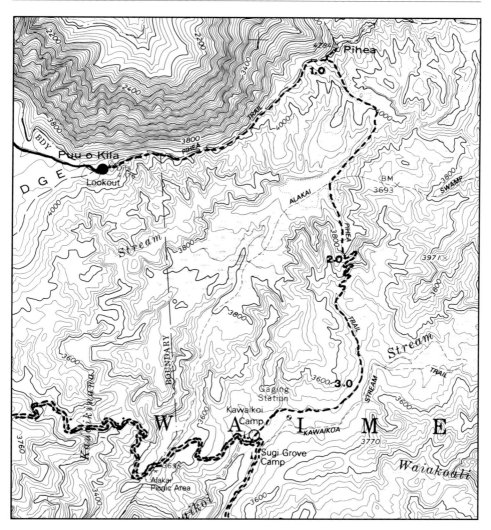

trees. From this point on, the trail condition improves. At 2.0 miles the Pihea Trail makes a switchbacking descent to a branch of Kawaikoi Stream. At about 3.2 miles, after crossing a small stream, the trail passes by a fair-weather ford leading across Kawaikoi Stream to the Kawaikoi Stream Trail. The Pihea Trail does not cross but continues down the northwest side of Kawaikoi Stream to end at Kawaikoi Camp.

Good overnight tent camping by permit is available at Kawaikoi Camp, which is 3.7 miles down Mohihi Road from Highway 550, and at Sugi Grove Campground, 0.2 miles further down Mohihi Road and across a fair-weather ford of Kawaikoi Stream.

Halemanu and Kumuwela Roads

All of the trailheads for the trails described in this section are within fairly short walking distance down the dirt roads starting near the Kokee State Park Campground, Kokee Lodge, and Park Headquarters. This is important since the 4-wheel-drive roads in the area can be difficult to drive at best. They may be impossible to drive if wet, since the cohesive, fine-grained soils in the area become extremely slick. A light rain can make them undriveable. The less the roads are maintained, however, the better they are for hiking. It is usually better to walk them in any event since they go through landscape that is best appreciated at a leisurely pace. Mileage walked along the roads should, of course, be added to the trail mileage to figure total hiking distance.

Halemanu Road, which starts 1.3 miles down Highway 550 from Park Headquarters, leads to the trailheads for the Cliff, Canyon and Black Pipe Trails. It is also the terminus of the Halemanu-Kokee Trail.

Kumuwela Road, which starts 0.1 miles up Highway 550 from Kokee State Park Headquarters, leads down to Camp Sloggett and eventually joins Mohihi (Camp 10) Road. Along it or on one of its side roads start four of the trails described in this section: the Halemanu-Kokee, Waininiua, Kumuwela, and Puu Kaohelo (Berry Flat) Trails.

Koa Forest

Faye Road, which starts about 0.4 miles down Highway 550 from Park Headquarters, leads only to Unnamed Trail. This useful, though short, trail connects Faye Road to Halemanu Road, considerably shortening the walking access from Park Headquarters to the trails along Halemanu Road and making it easy to make several loop trips.

These interconnecting trails and primitive roads can be linked up like beads on

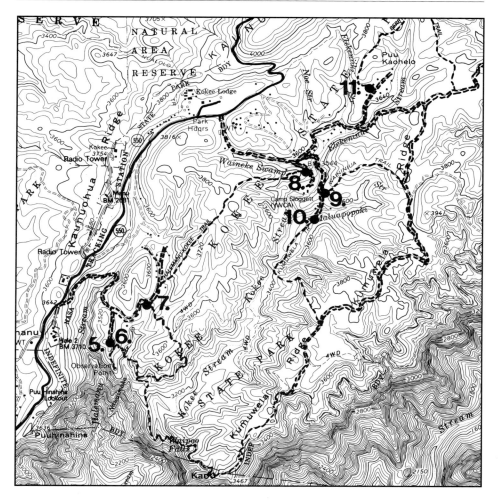

a string or verses of Persian poetry to offer variety. Short loops and long loops can be made up to fit ones's fancy and interests. A variety of combinations are mentioned in the trail descriptions but careful study of the maps will suggest others. There is no camping located along these day-hiking trails, but they can be hiked nicely using Kokee State Park Campground, Kokee Lodge, or Camp Sloggett as base areas.

5. Cliff

Halemanu and Kumuwela Roads

0.4 hours, round trip
50 calories; easiest
0.4 miles, round trip
Highest point: 3540 feet
Lowest point: 3450 feet
Maps: Makaha Point, Haena
Division of State Parks

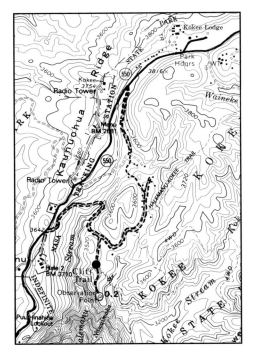

This short, easy trail provides a view of another aspect of Waimea Canyon. It leads to a spot with a commanding view of the early morning and late afternoon light and shadows playing on the canyon walls. Goats may often be seen browsing nearby at dawn. These creatures were first introduced to the islands through the misguided generosity of early European sea captains. With their broad and bottomless appetites and incredible climbing skills the goats have taken a terrible toll on the native species of plants and leave the land bare for erosion. Goats eat everything, everywhere.

Route: From Kokee State Park Headquarters go 1.3 miles down Highway 550 towards Waimea to the park entrance sign reading "Kokee State Park." The turnoff is just below the sign, on the east side of the road, toward Waimea Canyon. At the turnoff, a paved driveway leads up to a NASA facility and 4-wheel-drive Halemanu Road leads down, left, toward the trailhead. This dirt road is undriveable if wet and therefore it is best to park here. The trailhead is only a 0.8-mile walk along Halemanu Road. If you walk the road, add the distance to the trail mileage. Halemanu Road descends, crosses tiny Halemanu Stream, and, at 0.6 miles, reaches the first turn-off, right, onto an unnamed dirt road. Take this spur road 0.2 miles to its end at a small parking area from which both the Cliff and Canyon Trails start.

As an alternative, the trailhead can be reached from Kokee Park Headquarters by walking 0.4 miles down Highway 550 to Faye Road, the first dirt road on the left. Follow Faye Road down 0.4 miles to where it splits right and left. Take the trail, which goes straight ahead (the Unnamed Trail), and follow it 0.2 miles to Halemanu Road. At 0.5 miles along Halemanu Road and shortly before coming to Halemanu Stream, the unnamed spur road leads off on the left side of the

View from the Cliff Trail

road. The trailhead is 0.2 miles down the spur road.

The Cliff and the Canyon Trails start at the same trailhead. The joint trail goes 50 yards and then splits into two separate trails with the Cliff Trail leading to the right. From the fork it first climbs gently and then levels off. As the trail nears its end, a metal railing follows along it to the viewpoint overlooking Waimea Canyon to the south and west. An eroded unmaintained trail, going nowhere in particular, leads down from the lookout onto the ridge below. In the early morning goats can be seen grazing along the ridge.

6. Canyon
Halemanu and Kumuwela Roads
4 hours, round trip
800 calories; harder
4.8 miles, round trip
Highest point: 3650 feet
Lowest point: 3030 feet
Maps: Haena, Makaha Point,
      Waimea Canyon
Division of State Parks

A fine view down the length of Waimea Canyon all the way to the sea is the principal attraction of this trail, which skirts along the Canyon's north rim. A ginger-fringed pool along the route is a pleasant addition. Along the trail is evidence of the changes taking place in the landscape as native plants are overwhelmed by introduced species such as Himalayan blackberry (*Rubus discolor*) and lantana (*Lantana camara*).

Route: From Kokee State Park Head-quarters go 1.3 miles back down Highway 550 towards Waimea to the park entrance sign reading "Kokee State Park." The turnoff is just below the sign, on the east side of the road, towards Waimea Canyon. At the turnoff, a paved driveway leads up to a NASA facility and 4-wheel-drive Halemanu Road leads down, left, toward the trailhead. This dirt road is undriveable if wet and therefore it is best to park here. The trailhead is only a 0.8 mile walk along Halemanu Road. If you walk the road, add the distance to the trail mileage. The road descends, crosses tiny Halemanu Stream, and at 0.6 miles reaches a turn-off, right, onto an unnamed dirt road. Take this spur road 0.2 miles to its end and the start of the Cliff and Canyon Trails.

As an alternative, the trailhead can be reached from Kokee Park Headquarters by walking 0.4 miles down Highway 550 to Faye Road, the first dirt road on the left. Follow Faye Road down 0.4 miles to

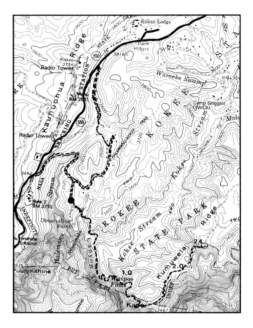

where it splits right and left. Take the trail, which goes straight ahead (Unnamed Trail), and follow it for 0.2 miles to Halemanu Road. At 0.5 miles along Halemanu Road and shortly before coming to Halemanu Stream, an unnamed spur road leads off on the left side of the road. The trailhead is at a small parking area 0.2 miles down the spur road.

The Canyon and Cliff Trails start at the same trailhead. The joint trail descends for 50 yards and then splits into two separate trails with the Canyon Trail leading to the left. From the fork the Canyon Trail

View down Waimea Canyon

switchbacks steeply down through remnants of a native koa forest blown down by Hurricane Iwa in 1982. As it reaches the bottom of the first valley it passes above an exposed portion of an irrigation ditch and tunnel system. It then climbs and reaches a junction with the Black Pipe Trail coming in from the left at 0.4 miles.

The Canyon Trail leads down onto a broad, bare ridge providing a panoramic vista of the high cliffs of Waimea Canyon to the west and south. In the still, early morning, when the views are best, one may hear the sounds of goats and birds in the distance. Beware the small round rocks on the hard surface, which could roll like ball bearings causing a fatal slip. The trail continues down off the eroded ridge southeast toward the sound of Kokee Stream's Waipoo Falls amid a grove of koa trees in a lush dell at 0.8 miles. A short spur trail leads left, upstream, to the delightful falls and spacious pool surrounded by ginger, koa, ohia, passion flower, kukui, and hala. The main trail continues right, crossing the stream at the top of a smaller, lower falls. It then leads up the grass covered hillside

to contour generally east, above the canyon cliffs.

Along the way the trail passes through native koa forests being overwhelmed by blackberry, lantana, and aggressive grass. Silky oak trees and groves of planted Australian eucalyptus seem to hold their own. On this land the ancient plant communities were ravaged by introduced goats, exposing the soil to erosion and invasion by introduced plants. These plants have displaced the rare native plants; however, they have the virtue of better withstanding the goats and, thus, saving the soil from erosion.

At about one and a half miles the trail reaches the ridge overlooking both Waimea and Poomau Canyons. From there one may see the graceful white-tailed tropic birds and flights of dragonfly-like helicopters skirting the cliffs below. The trail levels out as it reaches its end at 2.4 miles on the broad expanse of Kumuwela Lookout at the end of Kumuwela Road.

It is possible to continue on by walking along Kumuwela Road to the Kumuwela Trail and thus make a loop trip back to Park Headquarters.

7. Black Pipe
Halemanu and Kumuwela Roads
1½ hours, round trip
250 calories; easier
1.6 miles, round trip
Highest point: 3575 feet
Lowest point: 3320 feet
Maps: Haena, Waimea Canyon
Division of State Parks

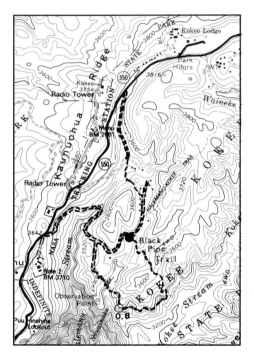

This easy trail is used principally as a connector trail to the Canyon Trail. The trail leads part of the way along the side of the valley of Kokee Stream. Shortly before it meets the Canyon Trail, the trail offers good views of Waimea Canyon and the opportunity to see specimens of the rare iliau plant.

Route: From Kokee State Park Headquarters go down Highway 550 towards Waimea for 1.3 miles to the park entrance sign reading "Kokee State Park." The turnoff is just below the sign, on the east side of the road, towards Waimea Canyon. At the turnoff, a paved driveway leads up to a NASA facility and 4-wheel-drive Halemanu Road leads down, left, toward the trailhead. This dirt road is undriveable if wet and therefore it is best to park here. The trailhead is only a 0.8 mile walk along Halemanu Road. If you walk the road, add the distance to the trail mileage. Halemanu Road descends and crosses tiny Halemanu Stream. Continue on to the second spur road on the right. This turnoff is considered to be the trailhead.

As an alternative, the trailhead can be reached from Kokee Park Headquarters by walking 0.4 miles down Highway 550 to Faye Road, the first dirt road on the left. Follow Faye Road down 0.4 miles to where it splits right and left. Take the trail, which goes straight ahead (Unnamed Trail), and follow it 0.2 miles to Halemanu

Road. At 0.3 miles along Halemanu Road a spur road leads to the left. This turnoff is the trailhead.

Hike the trail (dirt road) descending first toward the southeast. The trail then climbs the hillside until it reaches the crest of a ridge at 0.3 miles. There the remnants of an abandoned side road descend steeply down, easterly, while the main road contours left. Follow the descending remnant side road. The side road soon becomes a trail contouring

Along the Black Pipe Trail

down along the hillside above Kokee Stream through eucalyptus and grass. It then switchbacks down toward the ginger-lined stream, but before reaching it, the trail contours around to the west, providing views of Waimea Canyon.

After the trail contours to the west it passes above a group of rare iliau plants (*Wilkesia gymnoxiphium*) growing on a harsh site. The iliau has a single woody stem and whorl of narrow leaves at the top, collecting together at the stem. The Black Pipe Trail joins the Canyon Trail after 0.8 miles. Instead of returning the same way, a loop can be made by returning via the Canyon Trail.

8. Halemanu–Kokee
Halemanu and Kumuwela Roads
1½ hours, round trip
400 calories; easier
2.4 miles, round trip
Highest point: 3790 feet
Lowest point: 3500 feet
Map: Haena
Division of State Parks

This trail is close to Kokee Park Head-quarters and may be reached easily by walking down Kumuwela Road even when it is undriveable. It may be hiked in conjunction with several other trails described in this section. The native koa forest through which it passes was severe-ly damaged by Hurricane Iwa in 1982. Trees were toppled or stripped of their leaves and branches by winds exceeding 100 miles per hour. The increased sunlight to the blackberries, lantana and other intro-duced plants allowed them to thrive. These aggressive plants suppress koa seedlings, and will, therefore, eventually destroy the forest. Such a sorry sight shows the wis-dom of Hawaii's stringent controls on importation of plants and animals.

Route: From Kokee Park Headquarters go 0.1 miles up Highway 550 to Kumuwela Road on the right side of the Highway. This 4-wheel-drive dirt road is undriveable if wet. Add road mileage to the hike if you walk the road. Proceed 0.5 miles down Kumuwela Road to the first turnoff on the right leading to Camp Sloggett. If you are driving, park there. The trailhead is 0.1 miles down the turnoff, on the right side of the road.

The trail climbs gently through an under-story of grass and blackberries. As it nears a ridgetop, it passes through a dying koa for-est, overtopped with passion flower vines and crowded by lantana and blackberries. The trail then descends to meet Halemanu

Hard working trail crew

Road about one mile from the trailhead.

By turning left on Halemanu Road a variety of loop trips can be made by com-bining the road with other trails in the area. A shorter loop returning to Kokee can be made by turning right on Halemanu Road and continuing for 0.1 miles to its end. There, the 0.2-mile long Unnamed Trail leads off to the left, cross-ing a small stream, and soon reaching Faye Road. This dirt road leads uphill and meets Highway 550 at 0.4 miles. Park Headquarters is 0.4 miles to the right.

Fallen Giants

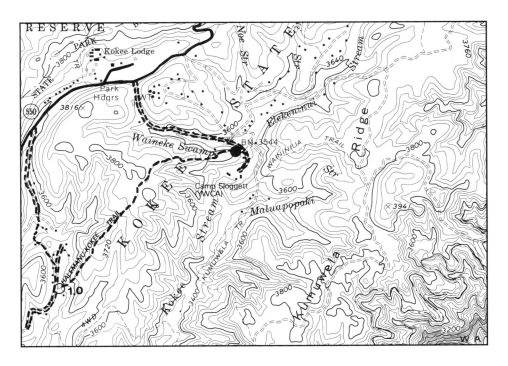

9. Waininiua

Halemanu and Kumuwela Roads
⅔ hours, round trip
150 calories; easier
1.0 mile, round trip
Highest point: 3800 feet
Lowest point: 3570 feet
Map: Haena
Division of State Parks

The Waininiua Trail is a short trail good for bird watching and observing the succession of introduced species into the native ohia lehua and koa forest. In this area of upland forest, endemic birds are still fairly numerous. Though much has been lost from their habitat, the endemic ohia lehua and koa forest, much remains. This is unlike most lowland regions where virtually all the original flora has been replaced by introduced species, dooming the original birds to extinction. Furthermore, mosquitoes which may spread diseases do not range as high in elevation as Kokee.

It is hard to get a good look at the birds because they are generally smaller than five inches long and move quickly. Usually all that is seen is a flash of red, yellow, or brown as you move through an open patch of forest. However, their calls can be heard all around. The apapane, a red bird with a fairly straight beak, seems to have a multitude of calls. The iiwi, also red, but with a curved beak, has a loud, raucous call. The anianiau is yellow-green with a two-note call. The elepaio is mostly brown, with white on its tail, and makes merry whistles and chirps. The best time to observe and hear the birds is early morning.

The loud crowing heard in the forest is from the colorful moa, a jungle fowl, introduced by the Polynesians and once found in all the islands. The birds perch in trees at night, but nest on the ground. This would make them vulnerable to extermination by the mongoose. ForZtunately, the mongoose was not successfully introduced into Kauai, unlike the other islands. So the story goes: the crate of mongooses shipped to Kauai contained a particularly ill-tempered one, which, not understanding the golden opportunities awaiting it, unkindly bit the dock worker handling the crate. The injured man, with suddenly enhanced ecological awareness, immediately drowned the lot of them, sparing much wildlife on Kauai from extinction.

Route: From Kokee State Park Headquarters go up Highway 550 to Kumuwela Road at 0.1 miles on the right side of the highway. This 4-wheel-drive dirt road is undriveable if wet. If you walk the road, add the distance to the trail mileage. Continue down Kumuwela Road for 0.5 miles to the second turnoff on the right, which is immediately after the turnoff to Camp Sloggett. If you are driving, it is best to park at the junction. Walk this primitive road, crossing over Kokee Stream upstream of a water intake and past several homes surrounded by lovely gardens. The trailhead is located on the left, on a downhill section of the road, 0.2 miles after crossing Kokee Stream.

The trail climbs 30 feet into the forest, then turns north and climbs gently by koa forest on the right and through occasional

Kokee Stream and Water Intake

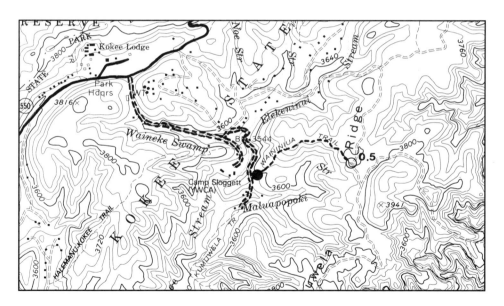

incursions of kahili ginger and blackberries. It starts to climb more steeply, and, as it levels out, begins to arch more and more easterly and then southeasterly. The trail passes into native ohia lehua forest with incursions of guava. It ends after half a mile when it reaches Kumuwela Road.

You may return by turning right onto Kumuwela Road and continuing on it to the Kumuwela Trail for a loop trip. Another alternative for a longer hike is to continue on to the end of Kumuwela Road and return via the Canyon Trail.

10. Kumuwela
Halemanu and Kumuwela Roads

2 hours, round trip
350 calories; easier
2.6 miles, round trip
Highest point: 3800 feet
Lowest point: 3400 feet
Map: Haena
Division of State Parks

This trail provides good opportunities for viewing birds living in the lush foliage on the banks of Kokee Stream. Apparent along the route is the overwhelming influence of introduced passion flower, kahili ginger, and blackberry which are crowding out the endemic species.

Route: From Park Headquarters go 0.1 miles up Highway 550 to Kumuwela Road, which leads off from the right side of the highway. This 4-wheel-drive dirt road is undriveable if wet. If you walk the road, add the distance to the trail mileage. Continue on until you reach the second turnoff on the right at 0.5 miles and immediately after the turnoff to Camp Sloggett. If you are driving, it is best to park at this junction. Walk this primitive road, crossing over Kokee Stream upstream of a water intake. Continue on to the trailhead at the end of the road, 0.5 miles past the stream crossing, for a total of a little over a mile from the highway.

The trail leads up and down, generally southeast for about 0.4 miles, through dark, leafy woods and by dense stands of kahili ginger above Kokee Stream. In the more open sections, the smothering vines of the passion flower, introduced from Central and South America, drape the trees. The trail passes over a watercourse filled with kahili ginger and then begins to climb southeast, uphill, passing nasturtium and a vigorous grove of planted Australian silky oak. At about 0.6 miles

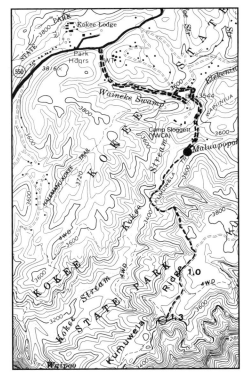

from its start, the trail reaches a plateau covered entirely with impenetrable masses of coarse, aggressive blackberry. By heroic work, trail clearing crews have hacked a straight path through this nightmare of ecological imbalance.

The trail meets Kumuwela Road at 0.8 miles from its beginning. Turn right on the road and follow it down 0.5 miles to Kumuwela Lookout. This segment of

Silky Oak Grove

Kumuwela Road to the Lookout is considered here to be part of the trail. The lookout provides views of Waimea Canyon and the ocean. It is also the terminus of the Canyon Trail, which leads in from the west. The Ditch Trail, east from the lookout, has been closed because of a dangerous landslide.

Instead of returning the same way, it is possible to make a variety of loop trips via the Canyon Trail or via Kumuwela Road and the Waininiua Trail.

11. Puu Kaohelo (Berry Flat)

Halemanu and Kumuwela Roads

1½ hour, loop trip
250 calories; easier
2.2 miles, loop trip
Highest point: 3800 feet
Lowest point: 3550 feet
Map: Haena
Division of State Parks

During the Great Depression, awakening concern about conservation coincided with the need to create employment in government projects. As part of such projects seedling sugi and coast redwoods were planted in the Kokee area. Sugi comes from Japan, where it grows into magnificent and extremely valuable trees. The coast redwoods are from northern California, where they rapidly reach immense size. The introduced redwood and sugi have grown quickly, un6troubled by their natural enemies, which they left behind. In contrast, the prominent endemic trees of the area, koa and ohia, are being steadily overwhelmed by competition from introduced species of plants and animals.

This trail leads first through a native forest struggling to survive against the competition of blackberry, kahili ginger, and a host of less visible but nonetheless hostile newcomers. The trail then enters an apparently thriving forest of planted sugi and redwood, which shade out the undergrowth. The success of the giant redwood is deceptive. The trees have difficulty setting seed and regenerating without the trigger of the shortening fall days of their original northerly homes. The long range futures of both the natural and the introduced forests are, for these different reasons, clouded.

Route: From Kokee State Park Headquarters drive 0.1 miles up Highway 550

Coast Redwoods — Planted in the 1930's

to Kumuwela Road, which leads off on the right side of the highway. This 4-wheel-drive dirt road and others in the park are undriveable if wet, but can be walked as an alternative. Add road distance to the trail mileage if you walk the roads. Measure mileage from the start of Kumuwela Road. Go down this dirt road 0.9 miles to the Puu Kaohelo turnoff on the left, ignoring all other turnoffs. Go up the turnoff 0.2 miles to the trailhead,

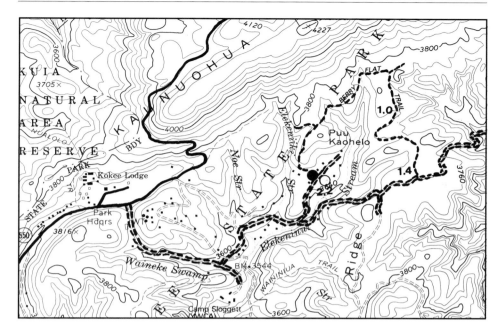

which is on the left, between two private properties.

At first the trail leads northwest, but after about 0.1 miles it swings right (north) while gradually climbing. After another 0.1 miles it splits into left and right hand branches. The trail to the left soon leads to a large ohia tree standing on stilt legs, possibly because it started its growth on a now-vanished tree fern. Beyond the tree, the abandoned trail soon becomes brushed over and impassable. Instead, take the branch to the right. The trail contours generally northeast through native ohia forest and introduced undergrowth, over wet, muddy areas to a sugi grove at 0.6 miles from the beginning of the trail.

About 100 yards after entering the sugi grove, a dead-end side trail leads ahead as the main trail turns to the right (south). The main trail passes open areas covered with uluhe (false staghorn fern) and by huge redwoods, some more than 13 feet in circumference. At 1.4 miles the trail reaches Mohihi (Camp 10) Road. Walk to the right for 0.6 miles to the junction of Mohihi and Kumuwela Roads and turn right again at the junction to Puu Kaohelo. To complete the loop walk up the spur road 0.2 miles to return to the trailhead.

Mohihi (Camp 10) Road

The five trails described in this group are all in the Na Pali-Kona Forest Reserve and start more than three miles from Highway 550 along 4-wheel-drive Mohihi (Camp 10) Road. This dirt road ends at day-use Camp 10 Shelter over six miles from the Highway. This dirt road and the access roads to it can be undriveable if wet, because of the cohesive, fine-grained soil underlying them.

Mohihi (Camp 10) Road can be reached by going down 4-wheel-drive Kumuwela Road, which starts at 0.1 miles up Highway 550 from Kokee State Park Headquarters. At approximately 1.3 miles from Highway 550, Mohihi (Camp 10) Road branches off to the left and Kumuwela Road continues to the right. Before reaching this turnoff Kumuwela Road may already be referred to by some as Mohihi Road or Camp 10 Road. At about 0.4 miles after the fork there is a "4-wheel-drive only" sign. Here the road starts down an incline which may be too slick to drive back up. Those who have driven this far may wish to park here.

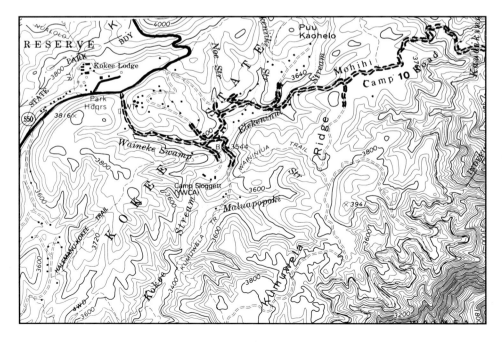

The best plan to hike these more distant trails may be to hike down Kumuwela and Mohihi (Camp 10) Roads to Kawaikoi or Sugi Grove Campgrounds which are on Mohihi (Camp 10) Road about 3.7 miles away from the highway. These campgrounds can then be nicely used as overnight base camps for hiking the trails along Mohihi (Camp 10) Road. Division of Forestry and Wildlife camping permits are required. It is also possible to use the Pihea Trail, which has direct Highway 550 access, as an alternate route for hiking the Alakai Swamp Trail.

Trail Sign at Forest Reserve Boundary

The Alakai Picnic Area, near the entrance to the Alakai Swamp Trail, offers pleasant views of the flat Alakai Swamp visible to the east. Five trails, all with trailheads along Mohihi (Camp 10) Road, are described in this section: Alakai Swamp, Kawaikoi Stream, Poomau Canyon Vista, Kohua Ridge, and Mohihi–Waialae. The Pihea Trail, described in the Highway 550 access section, ends on Mohihi (Camp 10) Road.

The trails have varying levels of difficulty, from the easiest to the hardest, and also have quite different terrain and views.

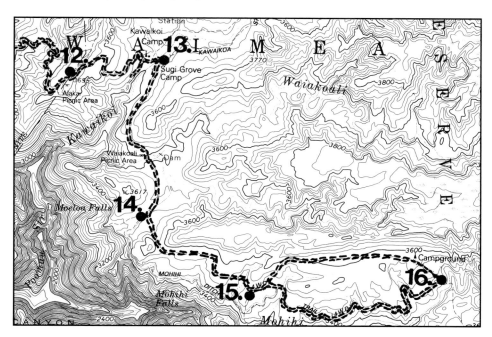

12. Alakai Swamp
Mohihi (Camp 10) Road
2¾ hours in, 2½ hours out
1350 calories; hardest
6.8 miles, round trip
Highest point: 4040 feet
Lowest point: 3700 feet
Map: Haena
Division of Forestry and Wildlife

The Alakai is the largest swamp in the Hawaiian Islands, covering about 10 square miles in the center of Kauai. It is almost completely surrounded by cliffs or rugged terrain. In it live some of Hawaii's rarest endemic birds and plants. This isolated area has been comparatively little touched by the outside world. Deep mud and poor forage have protected it from cattle, horses, sheep, and goats, but not, unfortunately, from pigs. All of the swamp lies above the upper limit of mosquitoes' range in Hawaii, about 3000 feet in elevation. Therefore, the endemic birds have been somewhat protected from mosquitoes, which may spread diseases.

The Alakai Swamp Trail, skirting just outside the Alakai Wilderness Preserve, provides relatively easy trail access to the north edge of the swamp. It was first laid out to construct a World War II telephone line, little sign of which remains. It ends at Kilohana viewpoint on the rim of the Wainiha Pali. The route becomes flat and featureless. As a result it may be easy to become lost, especially, since the area is usually exceedingly wet, cloud-covered, and rainy. Some places in the Alakai average 460 inches of rain per year.

It is best to hike the trail only during dry periods. Greater than usual caution should be exercised to stay on the trail. A compass should be carried and used. Confusing side trails made by hunters and wild pigs lead out periodically. If you stray

The Alakai Swamp

far from trail markers or the well-trodden path, it is likely that you have gone off the trail. Return to the last known point and start again. The Division of Forestry and Wildlife tries to keep mileage and tape markers along the way and is in the process of building a boardwalk.

Route: From Kokee State Park Headquarters, go 0.1 miles up Highway 550 to Kumuwela Road, a 4-wheel-drive dirt road on the right side of the highway. If wet, the dirt roads in this area are too slick to be driven, but can be walked as

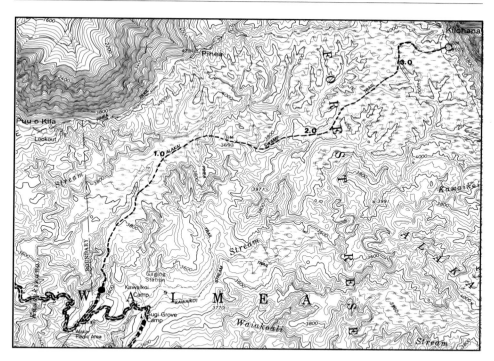

an alternative. Add road mileage to trail mileage if you walk the roads. As an all-weather alternative, take the Pihea Trail to gain access to the Alakai Swamp Trail.

Take Kumuwela Road for 1.3 miles to a fork at which Mohihi (Camp 10) Road branches off to the left. At about 1.6 miles, Mohihi Road reaches a "4-wheel-drive only" sign, beyond which the road becomes much worse and may be too slick for a vehicle to climb back up. At 3.1 miles, the road comes to the Forest Reserve entrance sign and the Alakai Shelter picnic area. From here a side road leads a little over 0.2 miles, left (north), to a parking area at the trailhead of the Alakai Swamp Trail.

For the first mile the trail follows the remnants of a 4-wheel-drive road used to install the World War II telephone line. The trail passes through the first bog before it crosses the Pihea Trail at 1.3 miles from the trailhead. At approximately 1.5 miles along the trail, after a steep descent of 200 feet in elevation, there is a fair weather crossing of a lovely branch of Kawaikoi Stream. This is a good lunch stop, a turnaround place for the less enthusiastic, and a good place to clean off mud on the return.

The route climbs up from the stream to the open bogs. Mist will quickly cloud camera lenses, and the air is so humid that it may be impossible to dry them off. Photographers should take along several lens filters. At almost three miles from the start, the route veers about 0.2 miles to the left (north). It soon returns to the course it was following and continues on toward the viewpoint at Kilohana, the end of the trail. From Kilohana one can see the Wainiha Valley below and the beaches at Hanalei, provided the weather is clear. The tree-covered Wainiha Valley compares to Waimea Canyon in size, but is seen by few people because of its inaccessibility. The return is made by retracing one's steps.

13. Kawaikoi Stream

Mohihi (Camp 10) Road

1½ hours, loop trip
400 calories; easier
2.5 miles, loop trip
Highest point: 3520 feet
Lowest point: 3440 feet
Map: Haena
Division of Forestry and Wildlife

This nearly level trail follows along the banks of the remote and lovely Kawaikoi Stream, one of the principal streams draining the Alakai Swamp. It is the habitat for many of the swamp's rare water fowl. These may be photographed with a telephoto lens, if approached quietly. The tannin from the luxuriant vegetation through which the stream flows stains its waters the color of tea.

Route: From Kokee State Park Headquarters go 0.1 miles up Highway 550 to Kumuwela Road, a 4-wheel-drive dirt road on the right side of the highway. If wet, the dirt roads in this area are too slick to be driven, but can be walked as an alternative. If you walk the roads, add road mileage to trail mileage. Measure road mileage from the start of Kumuwela Road. Ignoring all previous turnoffs, take this dirt road for approximately 1.3 miles to a fork at which Mohihi (Camp 10) Road branches off to the left. Follow Mohihi Road, which reaches a "4-wheel-drive only" sign at 1.6 miles from the highway. Beyond this sign the road gets much worse and may be too slick for a vehicle to climb back up.

Follow Mohihi Road until you are 3.7 miles from the highway. At this point you will reach Kawaikoi Camp and Picnic Area and a dry weather ford across Kawaikoi Stream. The trailhead is about 100 yards beyond the ford, on the left, across from Sugi Grove Camp. The trail starts in a dense, vigorous grove of Japanese sugi (cedar) and redwoods planted during the Great Depression. It soon nears the stream and continues east along the south (right) bank.

At about 0.7 miles from its start the trail passes by a ford to the Pihea Trail. The Kawaikoi Stream Trail does not cross the ford, but continues up on the south bank. At 0.8 miles the trail starts a loop, with the right hand branch side-hilling east away from the stream. It soon returns, continuing upstream atop a 40 foot bluff. The trail descends and makes a sharp left turn to a dry weather crossing near the bluff. After this crossing the trail turns back downstream on the opposite side. It closely follows the stream on slippery footing to a dry weather crossing back across the stream, completing the loop. Follow the trail back downstream to return to the trailhead.

Sugi Grove Campground, 0.1 miles further down Mohihi Road from the trailhead, is a quiet, streamside camping area in a dense grove of large sugi trees. It may be crowded during fishing season in August or September. Since the Kawaikoi Stream Trail is only a day hike, Sugi Grove, Kawaikoi Camp, and Kokee State Park Campgrounds are good spots for overnight camping in connection with hikes on this trail.

Kawaikoi Stream

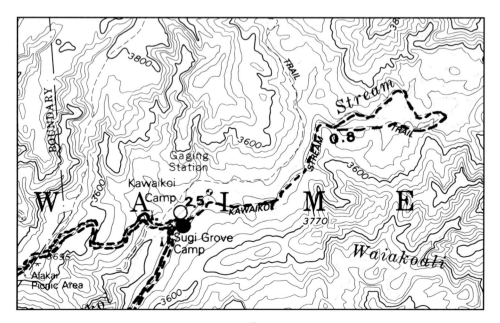

14. Poomau Canyon Vista
Mohihi (Camp 10) Road
½ hour, round trip
100 calories; easier
0.6 miles, round trip
Highest point: 3500 feet
Lowest loss: 3400 feet
Map: Haena
Division of Forestry and Wildlife

The sheer cliffs of Poomau Canyon, though most impressive, are rarely seen by visitors since one must walk to see them. Most people view Waimea Canyon from the lookouts on Highway 550 and leave it at that. The Poomau Canyon Vista Trail provides an additional vantage point for those wishing to see more.

Route: From Kokee State Park Headquarters go 0.1 miles up Highway 550 to Kumuwela Road, a 4-wheel-drive dirt road on the right side of the highway. If wet, the dirt roads in this area are too slick to be driven, but can be walked as an alternative. Add road mileage to trail mileage if you walk the roads. Measure road mileage from the start of Kumuwela Road. Ignoring all previous turnoffs, take this dirt road for approximately 1.3 miles to a fork at which Mohihi (Camp 10) Road branches off to the left. Follow Mohihi Road, which reaches a "4-wheel-drive only" sign at 1.6 miles. Beyond this sign the road becomes much worse and may be too slick for a vehicle to climb back up.

At 3.7 miles from the highway, Mohihi Road reaches Kawaikoi Camp and Picnic Area and a dry weather ford across Kawaikoi Stream. After crossing Kawaikoi Stream, the road leads past Sugi Grove, a quiet campground adjacent to the stream in a stand of tall Japanese sugi trees.

The Poomau Canyon Vista Trail starts

Trailhead and Norfolk Island Pine

at about 0.8 miles beyond the Kawaikoi Stream crossing (4.6 miles from the highway), shortly after the road crosses Waiakoali Stream. The trail leads off to the right of a 40-foot-high Norfolk Island Pine. It goes through a stand of sugi trees, across a small footbridge over an irrigation ditch paralleled by a dirt ditch road,

Poomau Canyon

and then into the native upland forest. It passes a wide variety of endemic plants, as it switchbacks down to the viewpoint above Poomau Canyon, where it ends. From the viewpoint you may see a great distance down the length of Poomau and Waimea Canyons and watch the graceful white-tailed tropic birds gliding on the winds near the cliffs below. Photography is best in early morning or late afternoon.

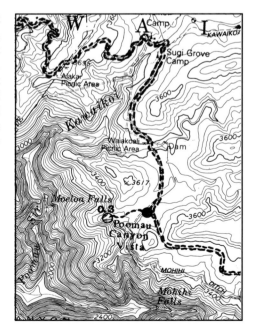

15. Kohua Ridge

Mohihi (Camp 10) Road

3½ hours, round trip
850 calories; harder
5.0 miles, round trip
Highest point: 3775 feet
Lowest point: 3220 feet
Maps: Haena, Waimea Canyon
Division of Forestry and Wildlife

This trail provides a panoramic view of Waimea Canyon from the end of Kohua Ridge, which projects toward the center of the Canyon. Go early in the morning to see goats, deer, and birds, which are relatively plentiful. The route crosses Mohihi Stream, a pleasant place for cooling off on the return trip.

Route: From Kokee State Park Headquarters, go 0.1 miles up Highway 550 to Kumuwela Road, a 4-wheel-drive dirt road on the right side of the highway. If wet, the dirt roads in this area are too slick to be driven, but may be walked as an alternative. Add the distance to the trail mileage if you walk the roads. Measure road mileage from the start of Kumuwela Road. Take this dirt road, ignoring turnoffs, for approximately 1.3 miles to a fork at which Mohihi (Camp 10) Road branches off to the left. At about 1.6 miles Mohihi Road reaches a "4-wheel-drive only" sign, beyond which the road gets much worse and may be too slick for vehicles to climb back up. Follow Mohihi Road past the Alakai Shelter picnic area at 3.1 miles and continue past Kawaikoi Camp at 3.7 miles. Drive over a dry-weather-only ford crossing Kawaikoi Stream and continue past the Poomau Canyon Vista trailhead at 4.6 miles. At about 5.4 miles Mohihi Road reaches the trailhead of the Kohua Ridge Trail.

The trail starts on the right side of the

View from End of Kohua Ridge

road and leads south, downhill, soon crossing Mohihi irrigation ditch and a dirt ditch road. It then descends fairly steeply to a dry weather crossing of Mohihi Stream at 0.3 miles from the start of the trail and about thirty yards upstream from where the trail first reaches the stream. After the crossing, the trail climbs, sometimes steeply, through a forest of sugi, ohia lehua, and koa to gain Kohua Ridge

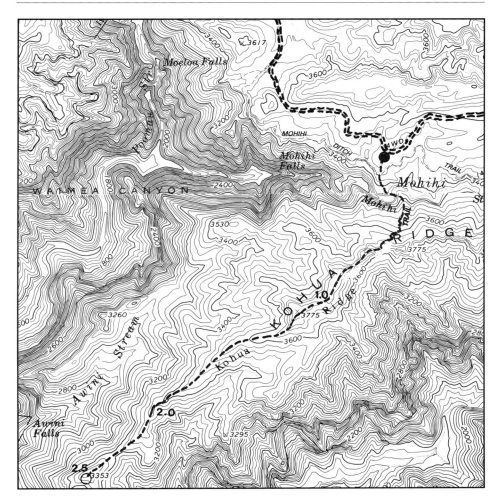

at 0.6 miles from the trailhead.

When it reaches the ridgetop the trail turns right and goes generally southwest on the ridge crest. The trail from this point is fairly level and provides good views of Koaie Valley to the southeast. On the ridgetop there is ample evidence of Hurricane Iwa of 1982 and its aftermath, the incursion of blackberries and undergrowth among the fallen native trees, which no longer can shade out these invaders. The trail dips and rises several times until it ends a little more than 2.5 miles from its start at a magnificent vista offering a panorama of the great cliffs of Poomau and Waimea Canyons. Beyond the end of the trail the eroded ridge drops off too steeply for further travel. Silky oak, pukiawe, iliau, ukiuki, aalii, a variety of grasses, and beds of white lichen are found along the trail.

16. Mohihi–Waialae
Mohihi (Camp 10) Road
7-8 hours, round trip
1500 calories; hardest
7.5 miles, round trip
Highest point: 4160 feet
Lowest point: 3420 feet
Map: Haena, Waimea Canyon
Division of Forestry and Wildlife

An idyllic swimming hole on Koaie Stream is the reward for taking this long, hard hike. The trail is at first easy to follow. It becomes increasingly confusing and difficult as it leads up into the fringes of the Alakai Swamp and then descends to end at Koaie Stream. There is much to see along the trail, including groves of thriving Sugi trees, broad views of Koaie Canyon, and an exceptional display of endemic and indigenous plants. The trail at one time continued beyond Koaie Camp all the way to Waialae Camp many miles away along Waialae Stream. However, it is no longer maintained and is now closed beyond Koaie Camp.

Route: From Kokee State Park Headquarters, go 0.1 miles up Highway 550 to Kumuwela Road, a 4-wheel-drive dirt road on the right side of the highway. If wet, the dirt roads in this area are too slick to be driven, but can be walked as an alternative. Add road mileage to trail mileage if you walk the roads. Measure road mileage from the start of Kumuwela Road. Take this dirt road for approximately 1.3 miles to a fork at which Mohihi (Camp 10) Road branches off to the left. Ignore turnoffs along the way. At about 1.6 miles from the highway, Mohihi Road reaches a "4-wheel-drive only" sign, after which the road gets much worse. Beyond this point the road may be too slick for vehicles to return uphill. Follow Mohihi Road past the

Alakai Shelter picnic area at 3.1 miles and continue past Kawaikoi Camp at 3.7 miles. Go over a dry-weather-only ford crossing Kawaikoi Stream and continue past the Poomau Canyon Vista trailhead at 4.6 miles and the trailhead to the Kohua Ridge Trail at about 5.4 miles.

About five and a half miles from the highway, Mohihi Road splits into upper and lower branches, which parallel each other at different elevations. The upper branch goes uphill and soon ends at the Camp 10 picnic shelter. From Camp 10 Shelter a path descends for 100 yards to cross the Mohihi Irrigation Ditch and reach a sign-in stand. The lower branch goes downhill to follow along the ditch to the Forest Division sign-in stand at the

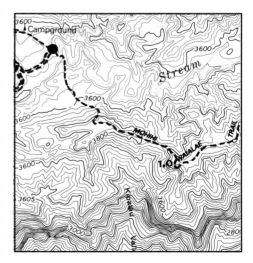

trailhead, which is next to the ditch.

From the sign-in stand the trail descends to cross a small stream, continues upstream a short way, and then branches off sharply to the right just before reaching a U.S. Geological Survey stream gaging building. The trail ascends through ohia trees, crosses a grassy swale, and then climbs through a magnificent stand of large Japanese sugi trees planted during the thirties. The trail switchbacks steeply uphill and attains the ridge, offering views of Koiae Canyon to the southeast.

At about 1.5 miles from the sign-in stand, just after reaching a rain gauge on a grassy knoll with encroaching blackberry thickets, the trail drops down somewhat to the right, southeast side of the ridge. The trail becomes much more difficult to follow after this because of encroaching vegetation. If it has not been brushed recently, it may be too difficult to proceed further and hikers should turn around and return. The trail keeps generally to the ridgetop, with occasional short descents around cliffs. Ferns become more and more plentiful as the trail reaches an arm of the flat plateau of the Alakai Swamp at about 2.7 miles from the start. The trail through the swamp fol-

Koiae Stream at the End of the Trail

lows a muddy, confusing course east through the rain forest, paralleling Koaie Canyon, invisible to the south.

At about 3 hours in and about 3.5 miles from the sign-in stand, the trail descends steeply 350 feet of elevation, down a rough, eroded, and sometimes grassy hillside. At last, the trail reaches its end at the lovely Koaie Stream and a pool with a 5-foot-high dike-formed waterfall.

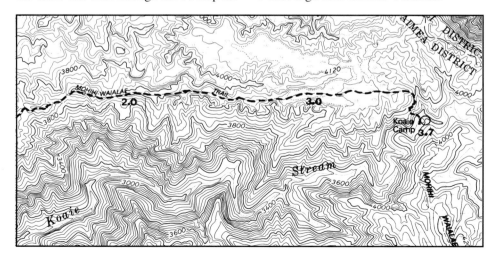

Waimea Canyon

Waimea Canyon, "The Grand Canyon of the Pacific," cuts up from the south along the flank of Kauai's ancient caldera and into its southeastern edge. It was probably formed when a fault crossed and captured several streams radiating down from the rain-drenched top of Kauai's ancient shield volcano. Several streams still radiate down from the high country of Kokee and the Alakai Swamp until they join the Waimea River, which flows south to the sea. Their canyons are visible from Highway 550 on the rim of Waimea Canyon. Waiahulu Stream drains most of Kokee Park, including Kokee Stream, which is close to several hiking trails. Poomau Stream, whose great canyon cliffs may be seen from the Poomau Canyon Vista, collects lovely Kawaikoi and Mohihi Streams. Waialae Stream plunges down impressive waterfalls into Waialae Canyon and then into Waimea Canyon.

The north and east sides of Waimea Canyon show the ancient Olokele Caldera, which is made up of thick, hard, nearly horizontal layers of ponded lava. The west side, on the other hand, is part of the side of the ancient shield volcano, and is composed of weak, thin layers of lava, sloping down toward the sea. The steep cliffs formed by streams cutting into these formations block access from the rim of Waimea Canyon to its floor and the floors of its side canyons. The stream courses are punctuated with waterfalls and the ridges are too steep for hiking.

Highway 550 follows along the rim of the Canyon and up the side of the ancient shield volcano from the coastal towns of Waimea and Kekaha. Along the way there are many fine views of the Canyon. The Canyon provides not only spectacular vistas from its rim but also fine back country hiking and camping along the streams on its floor. Only the Kukui Trail, dropping steeply down from Highway 550 on the west rim provides direct access to the Canyon floor. Koaie is the only side canyon that is accessible to any great extent and then only by hiking up from the Waimea River on the floor of Waimea Canyon.

The Kukui trailhead is quite accessible whether you stay at Kokee, Polihale State Park, or elsewhere on the island. The Division of Forestry and Wildlife maintains primitive shelters which can be used as base camps while hiking in the Waimea Canyon. Camping permits must be obtained from the Division of Forestry and Wildlife in Lihue.

View across Waimea Canyon

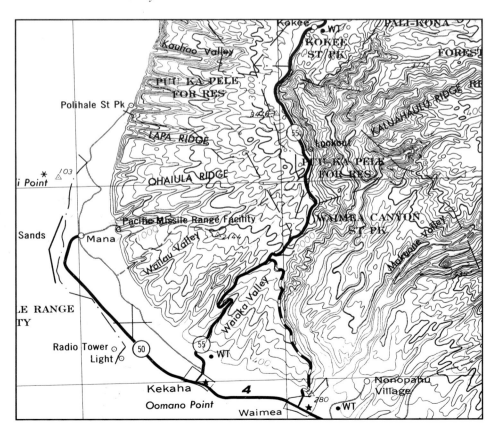

Canyon Rim Access

The Kukui Trail is the only direct public access to the trails in Waimea Canyon. This entrance into the canyon is on Highway 550 along the way to Kokee State Park. From the coastal town of Waimea, 50 miles west of Lihue, at Waimea Baptist Church take Waimea Canyon Drive to the right and follow it for almost seven miles to Highway 550. The trailhead is a little over two miles up from this junction. It is 6.8 miles down the Highway from Kokee State Park Headquarters.

Iliau Nature Loop, next to Highway 550 and on the canyon rim is a short pleasant trail for those not wanting to venture down to the canyon floor and up again. It offers grand views of the canyon and has along its course many species of endemic Hawaiian plants. Among them is a notable group of the iliau, a species related to the silversword of Maui.

The strenuous Kukui Trail descends 2300 feet from the canyon rim to Wiliwili Camp on the Waimea River. The Waimea Canyon Trail, which runs next to Wiliwili Camp, is the trunk trail following the Waimea River. Other trails on the canyon floor branch off of it. It is described here as an access trail to get from the Kukui Trail to the Koaie Canyon Trail.

For those wanting to spend more time hiking the trails in Waimea Canyon, overnight camping is possible at the Division of Forestry and Wildlife's primitive shelters next to streams on the canyon floor. There are five shelters:

Low water in the Waimea River

Wiliwili, Poachers, Kaluahaulu, Hipalau, and Lonomea. Wiliwili Camp, which is at the end of the Kukui Trail next to the Waimea River, tends to have the most traffic. Poachers' Camp is located half a mile from Wiliwili Camp down Waimea Stream and a quarter of a mile up Waialae Stream, but tends to be heavily used by hunters. Better sites are located upstream. Kaluahaula Camp is on the east bank of Waimea Stream, upstream about

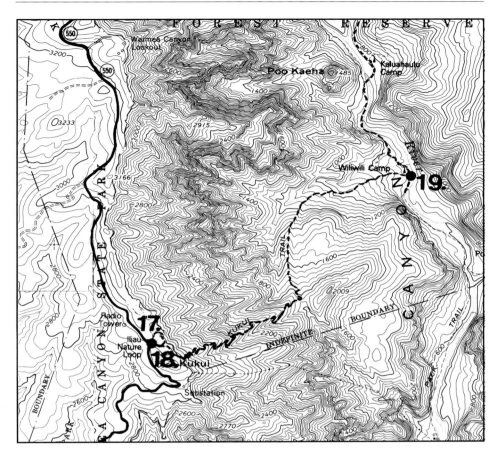

half a mile from Wiliwili Camp. About a mile further upstream is Hipalau Camp, on the east bank of Koaie Stream, and another mile and three-quarters upstream from there is Lonomea Camp.

The Division of Forestry and Wildlife will issue camping permits for periods of up to four nights within a 30-day period. The permits are available from the Department of Land and Natural Resources, Division of Forestry and Wildlife, P.O. Box 1671, Lihue, Kauai, HI 96766, telephone (808) 245-4444. Signing in and out at the trailhead is required for Forest Reserve overnight use area. See the Arrangements and Accommodations section for more details.

17. Iliau Nature Loop
Canyon Rim Access
¼ hours, loop trip
25 calories, easiest
0.25 miles, loop trip
Highest point: 2925 feet
Lowest point: 2900 feet
Map: Waimea Canyon
Division of Forestry and Wildlife

The Iliau Nature Loop, though short, is in a magnificent setting on the rim of Waimea Canyon. It can be reached immediately from Highway 550 and forms a loop at the start of the Kukui Trail. The trail surface is generally quite even and almost anyone can take it. Nearby is a delightful and little used picnic area with a day-use shelter.

Looking across Waimea Canyon toward the deep cut of Waialae Canyon, one may see a large double falls. Atop these falls stretches the Alakai Swamp. On the cliff face near the falls, thick, level basaltic lava flows may be seen. These ponded on the floor of the Kauai's ancient caldera, and are called the Olokele volcanics. These adamant layers of lava have resisted erosion and, thus, formed the plateau on which the Alakai Swamp has formed. On the west side of the canyon, where the trail is located, the lavas are of the Na Pali volcanics. These are thin lava flows that flowed down the side of the ancient shield volcano and, thus, are sloped at an angle. Structurally much less resistant to erosion and chemical decomposition, these have been deeply eroded by the action of streams.

Route: Take Highway 50 west from Lihue almost all the way through Waimea to Waimea Canyon Drive, which begins on the right at the Waimea Baptist Church. Follow Waimea Canyon Drive for almost 7 miles to Highway 550.

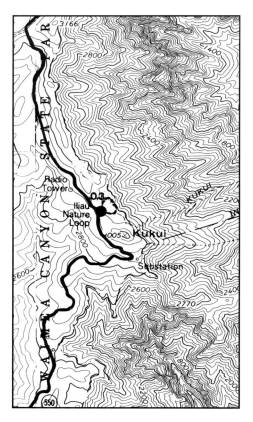

Follow it uphill to the right toward Kokee State Park. The trailhead is on the highway a little over two miles from this junction. It is 6.8 miles down from Kokee State Park Headquarters. Park along the roadside across from the trailhead.

The trailhead of the Kukui Trail and the Iliau Nature Loop are the same. Walk

Iliau Plants

about 100 yards to the sign-in stand near the canyon rim. Near the sign-in stand, the Iliau Nature Loop branches off to the left of the Kukui Trail. Along the trail are native upland plants. The trail is named after the most impressive of these, the iliau. Rare in most of the area, it seems to thrive here, perhaps because the presence of visitors frightens away the goats that plague the canyon.

The iliau (*Wilkesia gymnoxiphium*), a greensward, has a single woody stem and whorl of narrow leaves at the top, collecting together at the stem. It is a relative of the famous silversword (*Argyroxiphium sandwicense*) of Haleakala and the dwarf iliau (*Wilkesia hobdyi*) on the Na Pali Coast, all of which are probably descendants of the American tarweed, greatly evolved over millions of years in the Hawaiian Islands.

Continue along the rim of the canyon to a small rise with a spectacular view of the canyon. The trail loops around to return to the beginning, passing several, sometimes labelled, examples of endemic plants.

18. Kukui

Canyon Rim Access
1¾ hours down, 3 hours up
1600 calories; harder
5 miles, round trip
Highest point: 3925 feet
Lowest point: 650 feet
Map: Waimea Canyon
Division of Forestry and Wildlife

The steep Kukui Trail provides direct public access to the floor of Waimea Canyon, a strange and remote region of Kauai. It can be hiked in one day. However, the effort involved and the beauty of the canyon floor justify an overnight trip, especially with a side trip to Koaie Canyon. The climatic change from the often overcast and somewhat cool and wet top to the warm and dry valley floor 2300 feet below is pronounced. It is best to hike down at dawn when the abundant wildlife is most active. The return trip is also best made in the early morning when the sun's rays are cooler, since even at that time it can be an outstanding demon purge.

Most Forest Reserves are managed for day use only. In Waimea Canyon, where camping at the trailside is allowed, the Division of Forestry and Wildlife's present policy is to limit camping to four nights within a 30-day period. Camping permits must be obtained in advance from the Division's office in Lihue. Registration at the trailhead sign-in stand is required upon entering and leaving Waimea Canyon.

Route: Take Highway 50 west from Lihue almost all the way through Waimea to Waimea Canyon Drive, on the right at the Waimea Baptist Church. Follow Waimea Canyon Drive for almost 7 miles to Highway 550. Follow it uphill to the right toward Kokee State Park. The trail-head is up the highway a little over two miles from this junction. It is 6.8 miles down the highway from Kokee State Park Headquarters. Park along the roadside across from the trailhead.

Walk down the trail for 100 yards to the wooden sign-in stand close to the canyon rim. Beyond the sign-in stand the trail starts to switchback steeply down a ridge, toward Waimea River over two thousand feet below. The trail keeps close to the main ridgeline until it reaches a saddle where the ridge rises out to a small promontory. At this point the trail turns left (north) to go down a broad, eroded hillside. Near the bottom of the eroded area, the trail turns right, into the forest, and makes a switchbacking descent down to end at Wiliwili Camp. Wiliwili Camp is near the Waimea River where the Kukui Trail meets the Waimea River Trail. The Waimea River Trail, the trunk trail on the floor of the canyon, goes parallel to the river in both directions from the camp.

Water is unavailable along the Kukui Trail. Water from the river and from the trailside water seeps located a short distance downstream from Wiliwili Camp should be treated. There is a large swimming hole downstream from the camp.

Waimea Canyon

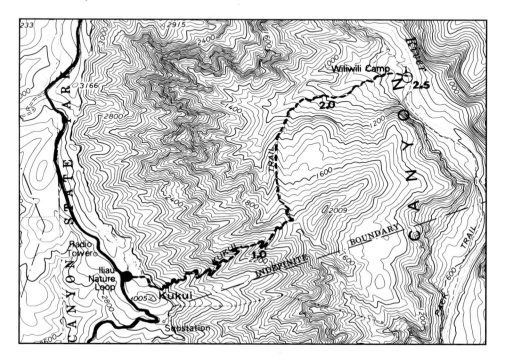

19. Koaie Canyon
(via 18. Kukui)
Canyon Rim Access
4½ hours, round trip
1000 calories; harder
6 miles, round trip
Highest point: 1440 feet
Lowest point: 650 feet
Map: Waimea Canyon
Division of Forestry and Wildlife

Koaie Canyon is one of the main side canyons off Waimea Canyon. Surrounded by high, steep canyon walls and with a large, boulder-filled mountain stream, Koaie Canyon seems like some alpine region far removed from the Hawaiian Islands. The canyon floor is quite warm and dry, while on the rim is the cool and continually rain-drenched Alakai Swamp. The stone walls and house foundations along the trail tell that once this was the home to many people. The lovely Koaie Stream offers excellent swimming holes and smooth rocks for basking in the sun.

Route: To reach the Koaie Canyon Trail you must first hike down the Kukui Trail to the bottom of Waimea Canyon. To be realistic about the difficulty of the hike, you must take this into consideration.

Having hiked the Kukui Trail to its end at Wiliwili Camp take the Waimea Canyon Trail upstream. It may be necessary to scramble along ledges above the river. About 0.6 miles upstream from Wiliwili Camp is a fair weather river crossing near the foot of Poo Kaeha, a castle-like, volcanic plug on the west side of the river. If the water is not too high, cross the river to the east bank. During stormy weather in the mountains, flash floods and high water make crossings too dangerous to attempt.

Proceed a short way up the east bank of the Waimea River, passing a small shel-

Canyon Wall

ter, Kaluahaulu Camp. Shortly upstream, the trail passes by a turnoff which leads across the Waimea River and further up Waimea Canyon. Continue on the right bank of the Waimea River to its confluence with Koaie Stream, which comes in from the right. The Koaie Canyon Trail leads up Koaie Stream along its southeast bank.

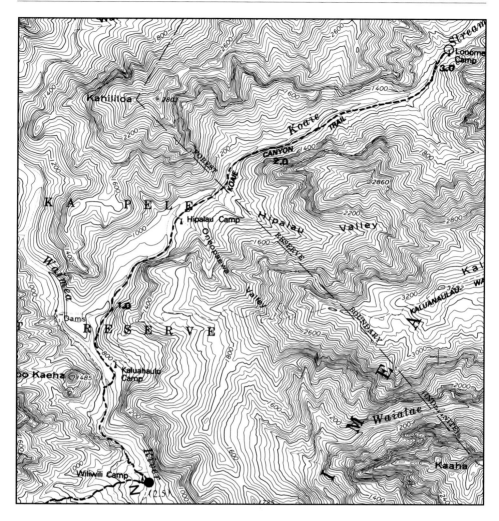

Close to the confluence of the Waimea River and Koaie Stream, the Koaie Canyon Trail passes by huge agave plants with their spiny, sword shaped leaves. It then leads into the forest between the stream and cliffs. The trail passes the shelter at Hipalau Camp about 0.8 miles up Koaie Canyon from the Waimea River. After passing by numerous stone ruins, it continues through dense thickets of kukui trees and guava. The trail ends at Lonomea Camp, 1.5 mile upstream from Hipalau Camp. A swimming hole and perches for leisurely sunbathing are next to the shelter.

Camping is allowed but limited to four nights within a 30-day period in the primitive shelters in Waimea and Koaie Canyons. Overnight camping permits must be obtained at the office of the Division of Forestry and Wildlife in Lihue. Registration at trailhead sign-in stands is required upon entering and leaving overnight use areas.

HIKING AREA NO. 3
East Kauai

East Kauai, now known for its many hotels, fine beaches, the airport, and the urban areas of Lihue, Kapaa, and Wailua, was once a center of Polynesian civilization. The complex of heiaus around the Wailua River evidences long occupation by the Polynesians. The Wailua River area was a particular center for the Hawaiian religion. The word, wai, in the Hawaiian language refers to fresh water and is often associated with the locations of priests and heiaus.

The whole region has a settled quality about it. Even the soils are of the oldest types found in the islands. The part of the shield volcano which once covered East Kauai was eroded down long ago. Ash and lava subsequently filled in the valleys formed by the earlier erosion, smoothing the landscape. The dependable rains, relatively level topography, and fertile soils account for the flourishing agricultural civilization of the Polynesians in this region.

The area is now a center of tourism and rightly so, since there is beauty on every hand. Less well-known than the fine beaches are the several good day-use trails in the area, with trailheads on paved roads. Hiking on these pleasant trails can be combined nicely with the amenities of the luxurious seaside hotels. For the thrifty, there are several Spartan hotels in downtown Lihue. There is no overnight camping along these trails.

Makaleha Mountains

This book describes three trails close to Wailua on Nounou Mountain, also called "the Sleeping Giant," and three in or near Keahua Forestry Arboretum in the Lihue–Koloa Forest Reserve further inland. All can be easily reached from the coast by paved road and hiked in a few hours. The trails on Nounou Mountain, a prominent landmark when looking inland from the coast, offer the more impressive

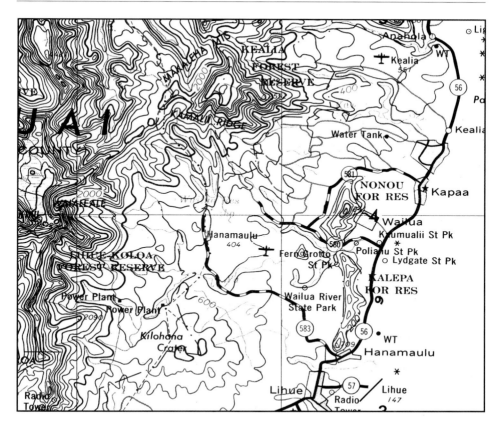

views. The trails in the rainier area a few miles inland pass through regions that still have much of the original Hawaiian plant life. These inland regions have an isolated beauty markedly different from the scenes on the coast.

Nounou Forest Reserve (the Sleeping Giant)

Nounou Mountain, about a mile and a half inland from the town of Wailua, looks like a "Sleeping Giant," when viewed from the ocean side. The mountain is on the north side of the Wailua River. The well-maintained trails on Nounou Mountain can be reached quickly from the nearby populated areas and resorts. There are three approaches to the mountain: a trail up the east side, a trail up the west side, and a trail, Kuomoo–Nounou, along the base of the west side leading to a junction with the west side trail. The east and west side trails join together at the top and soon lead to the end of the trail at a picnic shelter maintained by the Division of Forestry and Wildlife. The trails are for day use only. There are no campsites in the Nounou Forest Reserve.

If car shuttles can be arranged, two or more trails can be hiked together to make a grand tour of the mountain. If this is done, it is easier to start up either the Kuomoo–Nounou Trail or the Nounou Mountain–West Side Trail since they begin a little higher than the Nounou Mountain–East Side Trail.

The trails pass through open guava forest typical of that now found below 1500 feet on the wet sides of the Hawaiian Islands. The plants are mostly a collection of nineteenth and twentieth century newcomers, now naturalized. Guava, lantana, Spanish clover, and Norfolk Island pine are found along these trails. Plants brought by the Hawaiians, such as kukui and ti, are also in evidence along with a few endemic varieties.

Nounou Mountain is an extraordinarily inviting landmark. According to popular folklore the mountain is the body of a sleeping giant, turned to stone. Viewed from the mouth of the Wailua River, the skyline of the mountain does give support to such a theory. Imagination gives rise to the almost irresistible impulse to walk around atop the sleeping giant, always with a slight fear he might awake in irritation. Besides this, the views of the emerald bowl of the Lihue depression, the sunsets lighting the clouds atop Mt. Waialeale, and the changing twilight on the seacoast communities below are the chief attractions of hikes to the top of Nounou Mountain.

View of the Sleeping Giant across the Wailua River

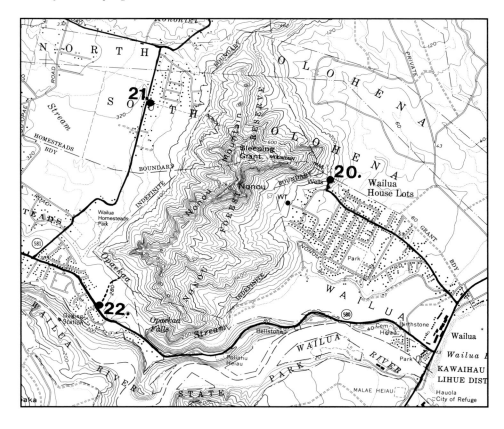

20. Nounou Mountain–East Side

Nounou Forest Reserve
(the Sleeping Giant)

2 hours up, 1½ down
600 calories; harder
3.5 miles, round trip
Highest point: 1120 feet
Lowest point: 120 feet
Map: Kapaa
Division of Forestry and Wildlife

This trail in the Nounou Mountain Forest Reserve is at its best at dawn or sunset. From the top of Nounou Mountain (also called the "Sleeping Giant") the light of the setting sun, playing up through Mt. Waialeale's ever-present clouds, can present scenes of splendor and infinite variety. The picnic shelter atop Nounou Mountain at the end of this trail provides a fine view of the sunset, which is at a little before five on the shortest day, December 21st, and at about seven-thirty on the longest day, June 21st. In the evening the open hillside on the way back offers good views of the changing light. Night falls so quickly in Hawaii that if hikers wait until sunset to start down, flashlights and care to avoid drop-offs will be necessary for the return trip.

Route: Drive north from Lihue on Highway 56 for 6.0 miles to Haleilio Road, which is on the left, about 0.4 miles past the bridge over the Wailua River. Turn left onto Haleilio Road toward Nounou Mountain and drive for one mile until Haleilio Road curves left near telephone pole no. 38. Take the blacktopped driveway on the right leading uphill to the Department of Water pump site. The trailhead is on the left, just before the pumping equipment.

The trail starts first among trees but soon leaves them and switchbacks up the broad brush and grass-covered hillside. After a little over 0.5 miles, as the hillside become steeper, the trail comes to the cliff edge on the south side of the slope. Here a side path leads steeply up along the edge, seemingly providing a direct route to the top. Avoid it. It leads to dangerous, steep ledges of crumbling rock. The correct route switchbacks to the right, north, across the slope, descending before it switchbacks up again through woods well to the northern slope. Eventually, it skirts cliffs and eroded areas of red soil — perils to returning hikers hurrying down in the dark — and leads west until it joins the west side trail.

As one trail, the Nounou Mountain–East Side and Nounou Mountain–West Side Trails continue climbing southerly to end at the shelter atop the Sleeping Giant. An unofficial trail, somewhat steep and exposed to cliffs, continues south from the shelter clearing in a scramble onto the giant's head.

Cliffside View of the Wailua River

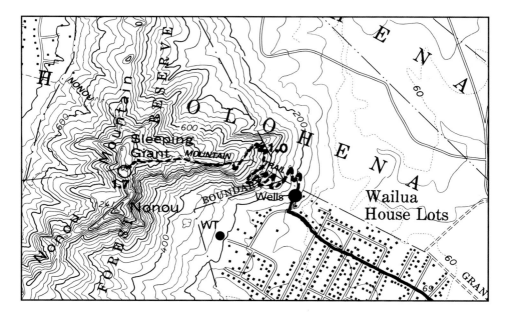

21. Nounou Mountain–West Side

Nounou Forest Reserve
(the Sleeping Giant)
1½ hours up, 1¼ hours down
500 calories; harder
3 miles, round trip
Highest point: 1120 feet
Lowest point: 325 feet
Map: Kapaa
Division of Forestry and Wildlife

Nounou Mountain, if viewed from the mouth of the Wailua River, does look like a sleeping giant, as it is sometimes called. His head is to the south, with a strong chin, a rather weak nose, and a somewhat protruding forehead. The trail from the west is the easiest route to the top. The Nounou Mountain–West Side Trail climbs through shady rows of Norfolk Island pine planted in the thirties — lovely, but home to murderous mosquitoes.

Route: Drive north from Lihue on Highway 56 for 5.6 miles to cross the Wailua River. Immediately take the first turnoff left onto Highway 580 (Kuamoo Road). Drive west for 2.8 miles and then turn right onto Highway 581 (Kamalu Road). Travel northerly behind Nounou Mountain for 1.4 miles to the trailhead. It is on the right, between houses, at telephone pole no. 11 on a 20-foot wide grassy right of way.

The trail leads almost due east, 500 yards, uphill, on a grassy pathway to the Forest Reserve boundary. As the trail enters the forest, the trail switchbacks left, then right, through thick guava. It soon reaches a grove of Norfolk Island pine and the junction with the Kuamoo–Nounou Trail, which leads south, while the Nounou Mountain–West Side Trail switchbacks east up through the pine grove. The trail then gains the north ridgeline of Nounou Mountain, where mosquito-relieving trade winds and views to the north and east lighten the hiker's spirits. The trail continues on to the east side of the ridge with good views to the eastern shores. At 1.4 miles from the start it joins the Nounou Mountain Trail–East Side. As one trail they continue up onto the ridgeline of the mountain, through guava and occasional ti plants, to end at a picnic shelter on the chest of the Sleeping Giant.

From the shelter Mt. Waialeale is visible to the west across the Lihue depression, a broad crater-like formation separated from the coast by Kalepa Ridge, to the south, and Nounou Mountain. From the shelter an unofficial trail, exposed to drop-offs, leads south through Christmas berry and strawberry guava to a scramble onto the chin and the head of the giant. The views of sunset at about five o'clock on December 21st, the shortest day, and at about seven-thirty on June 21st, the longest day, can be superb since the setting sun usually shines up through clear air to the permanent clouds atop Mt. Waialeale. If hikers stay for the sunset, they will need flashlights for the return trip. Night falls rapidly at this latitude.

Shelter at Trail's End atop the Sleeping Giant

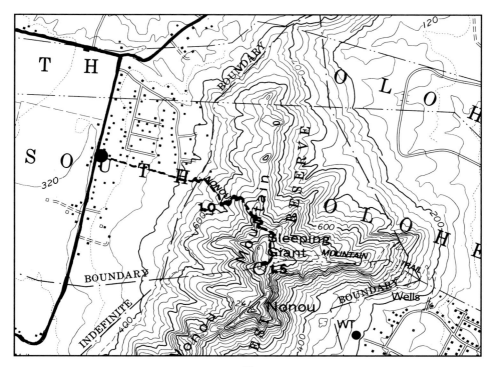

22. Kuamoo–Nounou

Nounou Forest Reserve
(the Sleeping Giant)
2 hours, round trip
500 calories; easier
3.7 miles, round trip
Highest point: 440 feet
Lowest point: 280 feet
Map: Kapaa
Division of Forestry and Wildlife

Good views of the valley of the Wailua River and of the spectacular sunsets over Mt. Waialeale are the best aspects of this trail. A picnic spot on a breezy promontory is the best vantage point. Beyond it the trail passes under tangled thickets of hau, by scattered hala trees, and through two vigorous stands of neatly planted Norfolk Island pine, eventually joining the Nounou Mountain–West Side Trail. The trail is suitable for jogging along its generally level, nearly two-mile course, contouring along the base of the west side of Nounou Mountain.

Route: Go north from Lihue on Highway 56 for 5.6 miles to the first turnoff on the left after crossing the Wailua River. Turn left onto Highway 580 (Kuamoo Road) and drive approximately 2.5 miles to the trailhead, which is toward Nounou Mountain on the right (northeast). At first the trail is level and goes directly toward the mountain, paralleling a row of trees to the west of the trail. It then crosses a footbridge over Opaekaa Stream. On the far side of the stream the trail immediately switchbacks left and then winds around a fenced area. It climbs up the mountainside, first toward the east, and then northwest until it reaches the promontory and a Division of Forestry and Wildlife picnic shelter after 0.7 miles.

From the shelter the trail contours generally northerly along the west side of Nounou Mountain, twisting in and out of gullies along the mountain's flank. The still of the forest is periodically broken by the sound of ripe fruit plopping down from the guava trees that have invaded the area. Toads occasionally cross the trail. Birds call out. Mosquitoes lurk in ambush. At about 1.4 miles the trail passes through the first grove of Norfolk Island pine. The trail follows close to the meadows along the Forest Reserve boundary. It swings somewhat toward the mountain shortly before it reaches its end at the junction with the Nounou Mountain–West Side Trail in a second grove of Norfolk Island pine at 1.9 miles. From this junction one may continue up the Nounou Mountain–West Side Trail to the picnic shelter atop the mountain, and then even choose to go down the Nounou Mountain–East Side Trail.

Picnic Shelter on Nounou Mountain

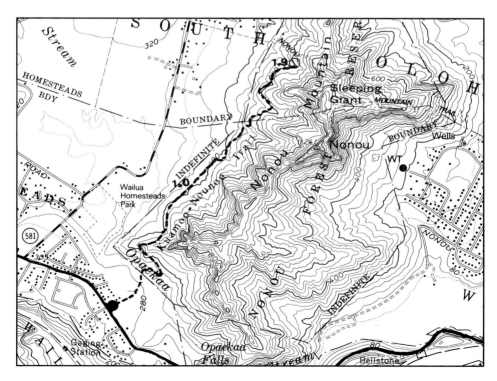

Lihue–Koloa Forest Reserve

The three trails in or near Keahua Forestry Arboretum pass through land covered with lush vegetation, encouraged by the ample rains and fertile soils of the region. Keahua Forestry Arboretum has a wide assortment of shrubs and trees in green and pleasant surroundings. A short, easy trail wanders through the Arboretum beside picnic spots and a lovely stream. The Kuilau Ridge and Moalepe Trails lead up onto Kuilau Ridge, a spur ridge of the Makaleha Mountains. The Moalepe Trail is the less interesting of the two in its lower portions. After meeting the Kuilau Ridge Trail, the Moalepe Trail travels a short distance into the rain forest with a wide assortment of endemic plants. The trail soon becomes too indistinct and brushed over to follow.

The upper regions of the Moalepe and Kuilau Ridge Trails reach portions of the original Hawaiian rain forest. Uluhe and amaumau, among other ferns, thickly cover the damp hillsides with a memorable richness of greenery. Vegetation crowds in on the trail. Clouds hang to the tops of the Makaleha Mountains. These steep mountains were formed from the remains of the side of the dome of Kauai's ancient shield volcano, now deeply eroded by surrounding streams. It is a land left to the rain and ferns, far removed from the people and activities of the plains below.

If a car shuttle can be arranged, the Moalepe and Kuilau Ridge Trails can be joined together by going up one and proceeding down the other. The trails in the Lihue–Koloa Forest Reserve are for day-use only; there is no camping in the area.

Lihue–Koloa Forest Reserve

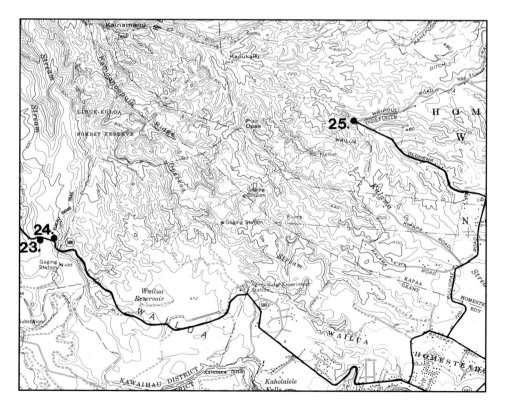

23. Keahua Forestry Arboretum
Lihue–Koloa Forest Reserve
½ hour, loop trip
100 calories; easiest
1 mile, loop trip
Highest point: 540 feet
Lowest point: 510 feet
Map: Kapaa, Waialeale
Division of Forestry and Wildlife

The plants in the Hawaiian Islands arrived during three time periods. Before the Polynesians, the rare arrivals of new plants were on the wind, by water, or as hitchhikers on or in animals. These plants evolved over millions of years to diverge into many empty ecological niches, creating unique species. Among the descendants of such early plants are the brilliant silversword, whose ancestor was some commonplace tarweed, and the ohia lehua with its bright flowers and multiplicity of forms.

Next, the Polynesians, arriving less than 2000 years ago, brought with them plants such as the kukui, milo, hau, and ti, all of which can be seen in the Arboretum. Finally, with the arrival of the Europeans, plants from all over the world were introduced either intentionally or accidentally. Prominent examples in the arboretum are the colorful Australian painted gum eucalyptus and the rose gum, which were planted for lumber.

Aside from these items of botanical interest the Arboretum offers a pleasant swimming hole and several picnic shelters with tables. The open lawns and quiet beauty of the place make it ideal for leisurely family outings.

Route: Drive north from Lihue on Highway 56 for 5.6 miles to cross the Wailua River. Turn left immediately onto Highway 580 (Kuamoo Road). Drive for 6.8 miles inland to the Arboretum, passing Opaekaa Falls on the way. The trailhead is on the left side of the road, just across the fair weather, concrete ford of Keahua Stream, which flows through the Arboretum. It is unsafe to ford in high water.

The trail first leads through a stand of green-barked gum trees. It soon forks. Follow the right-hand fork to ascend a small hillock, offering a good view of the Arboretum. From the hillock the trail makes a short, steep, and muddy descent back down to the stream. Proceed downstream passing through hau thickets in wet lowland forest. The trail ends at the confluence of two streams a short distance upstream of a stream gaging station. To complete the loop, return upstream along the trail, paralleling the stream. On the return loop the trail passes a swimming hole and picnic site.

Swimming Hole and Picnic Shelter

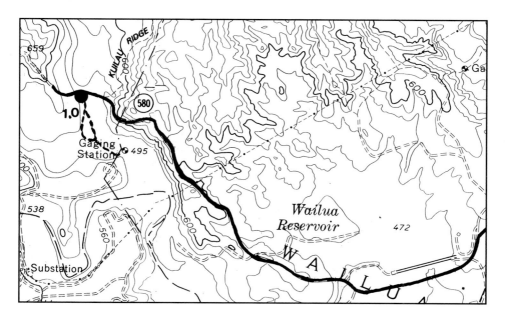

24. Kuilau Ridge
Lihue–Koloa Forest Reserve
3 hours, round trip
500 calories; harder
4.2 miles, round trip
Highest point: 1160 feet
Lowest point: 550 feet
Map: Kapaa, Waialeale
Division of Forestry and Wildlife

Plants flourish remarkably in Kauai's warm, wet climate. The Kuilau Ridge Trail in the Lihue–Koloa Forest Reserve leads up into progressively rainier areas, with the vegetation becoming correspondingly denser. The trail passes kukui trees, planted blue gum eucalyptus, and a host of smaller introduced plants before it moves into the fringes of the native fern and ohia lehua forest. The lower stretches of the trail pass by the usual collection of introduced plants, but the upper portions are covered with a lovely profusion of indigenous Hawaiian ferns. *Malabar Melastome*, a native of India, crowds out native plants. It does, however, have pretty pink flowers adding color to a native forest otherwise made up almost entirely of a great variety of shades of green.

Route: Drive north from Lihue on Highway 56 for 5.6 miles to cross the Wailua River. Immediately turn left onto Highway 580 (Kuamoo Road) and follow it westward for 6.7 miles until Keahua Forestry Arboretum comes into view. The trailhead is on the right side of the road

Shelter along the Kuilau Ridge Trail

about 200 yards before the Keahua Stream crossing. The trail follows the course of an old 4-wheel-drive road and is sometimes used by horses. It leads uphill, at first, east. It then turns north to ascend and follow Kuilau Ridge.

As the trail gains the ridgetop it looks down on tangled hau thickets and occasional banana plants in the valley of Kawi Stream, to the west. Along the way, disregard trails leading up from spur ridges to the east. At about 1.4 miles from its start the trail reaches a Division of Forestry and Wildlife picnic shelter with fine views. From the shelter the trail continues on a winding course up the ridge, through dense fern thickets, crosses a small stream, and finally reaches its end at an open area where the Moalepe Trail comes uphill from the right. The Moalepe Trail continues to follow the ridge, first dipping, then climbing uncertainly toward the Makaleha Mountains in the distance before it becomes too overgrown and difficult to follow.

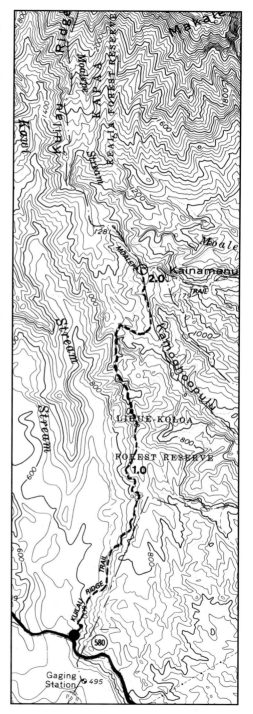

25. Moalepe

Lihue–Koloa Forest Reserve

3½ hours, round trip
550 calories; harder
4.6 miles, round trip
Highest point: 1325 feet
Lowest point: 575 feet
Map: Kapaa
Division of Forestry and Wildlife

The Moalepe Trail provides easy access to the edges of the dense rain forest atop Kuilau Ridge in the foothills of eastern Kauai's Makaleha Mountains. The first portion follows a 4-wheel-drive dirt road. Though not at first as attractive as the Kuilau Ridge Trail, it is pleasant, easy to follow, and shows the transition from a community of introduced lowland plants to the native fern and ohia lehua forest.

Route: Drive north from Lihue on Highway 56 for 5.6 miles to cross the Wailua River. Immediately turn left onto Highway 580 (Kuamoo Road) and follow it for 2.8 miles. Then turn right onto Highway 581 (Kamalu Road) and follow it for 1.7 miles generally north on the west side of Nounou Mountain until you reach Olohena Road. Turn left and follow Olohena Road for 1.7 miles to the end of the pavement, where Waipouli Road turns away toward the northeast.

The trailhead is considered to be this intersection. Park and hike the dirt continuation of the course of Olohena Road. This 4-wheel-drive dirt road following a right-of-way, crossing a pasture lease, in the Wailua Game Management Area. The road leads generally northwest through pasture and scrub land as it gently climbs toward Kuilau Ridge. Nearly all the plants and animals in this transplanted landscape are the descendants of introduced species.

The road comes to the Lihue–Koloa

Forest Reserve boundary a little over a mile from the trailhead (intersection) and then to a turn-around at about 1.5 miles. Vehicle travel is prohibited beyond this point and is soon nearly impossible. The route follows the deteriorating 4-wheel-drive track uphill and forks at about 1.7 miles. The tracks soon rejoin to form one route leading up toward Kuilau Ridge. Breaks in the heavy foliage occasionally offer good views down into the valley of Moalepe Stream.

The trail climbs past mud holes, into the fringes of the rain forest, which becomes progressively denser. At about 2.2 miles, the trail reaches a clearing at a junction with the Kuilau Ridge Trail coming up from the south. After this the Moalepe Trail continues to follow the ridge, first dipping, then climbing uncertainly toward the Makaleha Mountains until it becomes too overgrown to follow. If it has not been brushed recently it will be too wet and difficult to travel.

View near the End of the Moalepe Trail

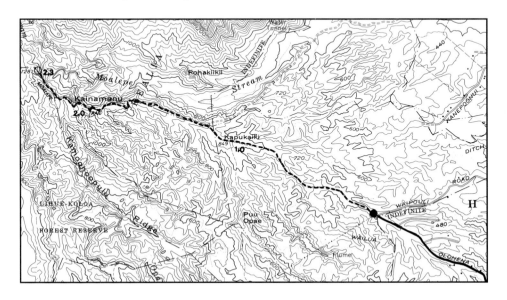

HIKING AREA NO. 4
North Kauai

Rain is the price of the lush beauty one finds all around on the windward side of Kauai. The abundant rain supports a dense guava forest with hala and kukui trees. Inland and higher, where there is yet more rain, the ohia lehua rain forest comes into its own. This is very much the garden area of Kauai, a land of streams, waterfalls, and plunge pools. It is reached from Lihue by Highway 56, which travels through some of the greenest land in the Hawaiian Islands.

The trails of the Halelea Forest Reserve are in or near the Hanalei Valley. This valley, one of the loveliest and rainiest in the Hawaiian Islands has long been a center of taro production. All parts of this remarkable plant are edible, if properly prepared. Oxalic acid crystals in the fresh plant make it poisonous until cooked; thus, it is usually quite safe from insects. When grown in paddies, taro is a remarkably productive crop and was the mainstay of large populations of Hawaiians. The Hanalei Valley Trail passes through country along the Hanalei River which was once covered with rice and taro paddies and is now overgrown with a profusion of nineteenth and twentieth century introduced plants.

Highway 56, which follows the north coast, is stopped by the high Na Pali cliffs at Haena. This is Hawaii's most famous wild coast, and rightly so. The Kalalau Trail follows along the cliffs to Kalalau Beach, 11 miles down the coast. Along the way it passes the lovely side valleys of Hanakapiai and Hanakoa, which have streams and waterfalls. Mercifully for hikers, the climate becomes drier as one nears Kalalau Beach. Beyond the beach the coast is too rugged even for foot travel. There are campsites at three locations along the Kalalau Trail. Division of State Parks camping permits are free but required.

The Na Pali Coast

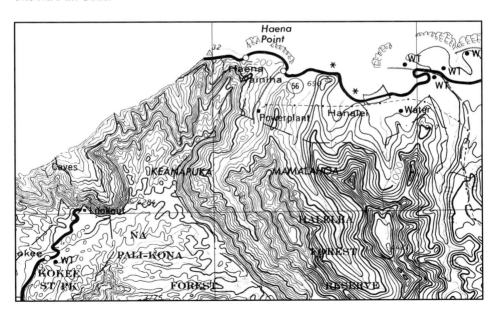

Halelea Forest Reserve

The Hanalei River is one of the largest in the Hawaiian Islands. In the alluvial plain at its mouth are paddies still used to produce taro commercially. The scenery gives some idea of the appearance of Hawaii's rich agricultural valleys when Captain Cook arrived. The Hanalei Valley Trail leads up along the floor of the Hanalei Valley, over abandoned taro land now covered with bamboo, mango trees, and a profusion of other introduced plants. Despite the abundant rain, the beauty of the lush foliage makes it well worth taking.

As the tradewinds, already saturated with water from the surrounding ocean, are forced upward by the abruptly rising mountains, they are cooled and are unable to hold their moisture. Heavy rains start at the coast, with about 75 inches of rain per year. The rainfall increases as one moves even a short distance up the Hanalei Valley. The three large valleys on the north coast, Hanalei, Lumahai, and Wainiha snare the tradewinds and bring them together at the summit of Mt. Waialeale, where rainfall well above 400 inches per year is the rule. This explains the surprising volume of the rivers, such as Hanalei, on the north coast, despite their small watersheds.

The Hanalei Trail is the only trail described in this area. The Okolehau Trail, not yet legally accessible and,

Noni

therefore, not described here, climbs out of the Hanalei Valley to a prominence overlooking Hanalei Bay. The Powerline Trail, which requires a permit from the Division of Forestry and Wildlife, is not described here either. It follows along the east rim of the Hanalei Valley and over the mountains to end near Keahua Forestry Arboretum near Wailua. There is no camping available along any of these trails.

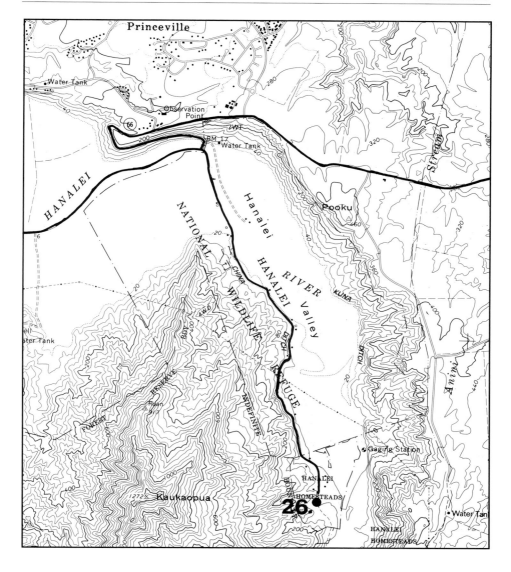

26. Hanalei Valley
Halelea Forest Reserve
1½ hours, round trip
300 calories; easier
3 miles, round trip
Highest point: 150 feet
Lowest point: 80 feet
Map: Hanalei
Division of Forestry and Wildlife

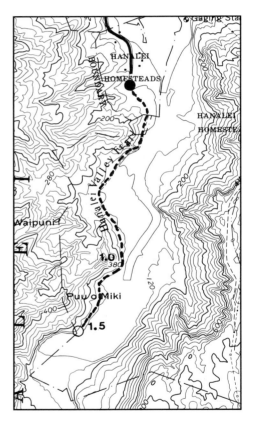

The area through which this route goes was once covered with fertile taro paddies like those now farmed farther down the valley. The taro provided food and a livelihood for the farming population that once lived in these areas. With more profitable opportunities elsewhere, most of the farming population in the region moved to urban areas. The land was left to encroaching bamboo, a collection of semi-tropical fruit trees, and massive mango trees. Expect generous portions of mud, rain, and mosquitoes along the trail.

Route: Drive north on Highway 56 for approximately 29 miles, continuing on past the turnoff to Princeville Resort for about 1.3 miles. Immediately after the bridge over Hanalei River, turn left onto Ohiki (Homestead) Road and drive for 4.2 miles to its end. The trailhead is about 50 yards from the end of the dirt road, between and beyond two houses. A sign-in stand is located at the trailhead.

The trail, which starts along the course of a heavily-rutted, undriveable, abandoned dirt road, heads south up the valley. The road begins to disappear as it reaches a grassy area. There the trail turns left, downhill, and passes by boulders. It then crosses a rapidly flowing small stream and gains the opposite bank with a short, sharp climb. It immediately turns left, downstream, and again right into a dense bamboo forest. Low rock walls evidence the once extensive taro farming.

The trail continues through the bamboo, crosses a gently flowing small stream, and proceeds through a mixed forest to the bank of the Hanalei River about a mile from the trailhead. This is a good turnaround point.

Massive, fern-covered mango stand along the bank of the river. There are

Hanalei River

good views upstream and downstream. From this point a faint trail continues upstream paralleling the river until it stops at the river. The course of the trail is subject to change because of periodic flooding and growth of brush.

The Na Pali Coast

The trails along the Na Pali Coast, on the northwest side of Kauai, are in many ways the best in the Hawaiian Islands. Along the way the hiker is presented with vistas of towering cliffs dropping down to the blue Pacific. The heavy waves restlessly pounding the coast show the ceaseless sculpting work of nature. Pandamus and kukui trees sway in the constant, warm trade winds. Clear streams lead down from near the summit plateau, spilling over waterfalls and through plunge pools to white sand beaches formed from offshore reefs. Best of all for backpackers, the land becomes drier as one approaches the Kalalau Valley.

The Kalalau Trail is the main trail along the coast, others lead inland from it. To reach the start of the Kalalau Trail, take Highway 56 north from Lihue and continue around the north shore past Hanalei to the road's end. The Kalalau Trail follows along the coastal cliffs to reach Kalalau Beach eleven miles down the coast. Sea cliffs prevent passage beyond Kalalau Beach even on foot. The rest of the coast is accessible only by sea or air. The Hanakapiai and Hanakoa Trails lead up from the Kalalau Trail into side valleys with lovely waterfalls and pools. Near the start of each of these trails and at Kalalau Beach there are camping areas for overnight stays. Camping areas are primitive and water must be treated or carried.

The Na Pali Coast is under the jurisdiction of the State Parks Division, which has done good work to preserve this jewel among hiking areas. Camping is limited to a maximum of five nights in a 30-day period in each State Park on Kauai. To further protect Hanakapiai and Hanakoa, camping is not permitted for any two consecutive nights at either site. Permits are free but required.

Campers must come in to the Division of State Parks office with proper identification for each person who is 18 years of age or older and sign the permit. Minors are not allowed to camp unless accompanied by an adult. Permits are issued during weekdays between 8 a.m. and 4 p.m. at the Division office in the State Office Building, 3060 Eiwa Street, Room 306, Lihue, Kauai. Permits may be mailed, if photocopies of identification for everyone camping are sent in.

Demand for camping along the Na Pali Coast is heavy, especially at Kalalau from May through September. Therefore, reservations must be obtained, by correspondence, preferably months in advance, from the Division of State Parks, P.O. Box 1671, Lihue, Kauai, HI 96766, telephone (808) 241-3444. The permit application must be received at least seven days prior to camping.

Hanakapiai Beach

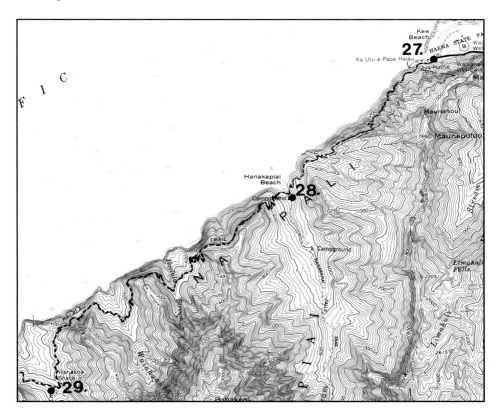

27. Kalalau Trail
The Na Pali Coast
2-4 days; 18 hours, round trip
4900 calories; hardest
22 miles, round trip
Highest point: 800 feet
Lowest point: sea level
Map: Haena
Division of State Parks

Balmy weather, massive cliffs, clear streams, and delightful, isolated beaches found along the Na Pali Coast make this trail one of the best in Hawaii. It is too exhausting and difficult for other than experienced hikers, especially beyond Hanakoa, where the trail is narrow and exposed to steep cliffs. To hike all the way to Kalalau Beach and back is a first-class adventure. However, even a short hike to the first viewpoints is amply rewarding for those who lack time to venture out further.

This long trail can be exceedingly slippery when wet. The seacoast has been heavily eroded by the elements which have formed the spectacular cliffs and valleys. The trail gradually becomes drier as it approaches the Kalalau Valley. Water from all streams and waterfalls should be treated. Obtain permits for all camping and for day use beyond Hanakapiai.

Route: Take Highway 56 north to its end at Haena State Park, 6.5 miles past Hanalei and about 40 miles from Lihue. The trail begins at a sign-in stand left of the parking lot at the end of the road. About 2 miles from the trailhead, the trail reaches the lovely Hanakapiai Valley. At the mouth of the valley there is a white

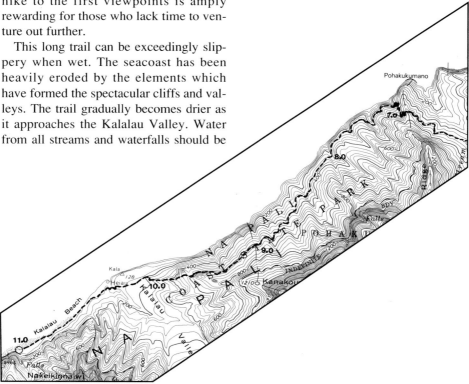

sand beach and a wilderness camping area of exceptional beauty. Shortly beyond the stream crossing starts the Hanakapiai Falls Trail leading to a side valley with a handsome waterfall and plunge pool.

The Kalalau Trail continues on, climbing steeply and crossing the Hoolulu and Waiahuakua Valleys before reaching the Hanakoa Valley, midway on the trail, and at about 6 miles. There are campsites and a

short path leads to a delightful swimming hole in Hanakoa Stream. The Hanakoa Falls Trail starts just beyond the stream.

At 9.5 miles the Kalalau Trail begins to descend toward the beach. It passes numerous stone walls, and a turnoff onto a secondary trail leading to waterfalls up the Kalalau Valley. Proceed along one of the paths paralleling the beach. The permitted camping area is close to the beach just inland toward its west end.

A small waterfall is located at the west end of the beach. Strong currents make the beach unsafe for swimming.

The Na Pali Coast

28. Hanakapiai Falls
(via 27. Kalalau)
The Na Pali Coast
3½ hours, round trip
600 calories; harder
3.5 miles, round trip
Highest point: 800 feet
Lowest point: 40 feet
Map: Haena
Division of State Parks

This lovely spur trail starting two miles down the Kalalau Trail leads into a sheltered valley, once thickly settled. Now only scattered, abandoned taro patches, stonework, and house foundations remain as evidence of former habitation. From ancient times the fertility of the soil and the abundance of water made the valley well-suited for taro production. Later, cash crops were raised. However, since the area was small and far from markets, such enterprises proved unprofitable. The trail passes the ruins of a small coffee mill, which used Hanakapiai Stream as its power source.

Cattle raising was attempted after the farmers left the valley, but this proved so destructive to the land that the cattle were finally removed and the land was placed under state administration. The scattered descendants of various cultivated plants now richly cover the valley floor. An occasional taro plant grows haphazardly next to kukui trees. Guava and mango offer their succulent fruit to passers-by.

Route: The trailhead to the Hanakapiai Valley Trail is 2.0 miles in along the Kalalau Trail, soon after it crosses Hanakapiai Stream. The trail follows up the west bank of Hanakapiai Stream, passing the ruins of the coffee mill. The trail is fairly easy for about a mile, but further on becomes increasingly difficult and crosses to the other side of the stream. Crossing points vary and the trail

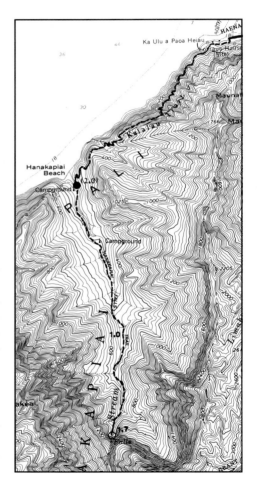

is poorly defined because of changes in the stream flow. However, the trail never strays far from the stream. If the stream is flooding, it is best not to continue since

Hanakapiai Falls

the upper crossings become progressively more difficult.

The trail leads by a series of small waterfalls and pools, ultimately ending at the main waterfall. A broad, deep pool formed by the falls provides ample room for a refreshing swim. Large stones surrounding the pool make fine perches for sunbathing. When swimming, beware of rocks swept down from the falls.

Camping is permitted near Hanakapiai Beach. Permits must be obtained during weekday working hours at the Division of State Parks in Lihue. Strong currents may make the beach unsafe for swimming, a fact established by several drownings.

29. Hanakoa Falls
(via 27. Kalalau)
The Na Pali Coast
1 hour, round trip
150 calories; harder
1 mile, round trip
Highest point: 800 feet
Lowest point: 470 feet
Map: Haena
Division of State Parks

This short spur trail starts six miles down the Kalalau Trail and is only half a mile long. It leads to a waterfall and pool, much like the Hanakapiai Falls Trail but has the advantage of being even farther off the beaten path. It is an enjoyable side trip for those hiking the Kalalau Trail or camping at Hanakoa. For those not having the time to do the whole Kalalau Trail, this is a good destination and turnaround point. A permit from the Division of State Parks is required for hiking this trail as for any camping or hiking past Hanakapiai Valley.

Route: The Hanakoa Falls Trail begins near the 6-mile mark on the Kalalau Trail about 20 yards west of the crossing of Hanakoa Stream. It goes up the valley, at first traversing the remnants of taro terraces close to the Kalalau Trail, then crossing the west fork of Hanakoa Stream. The trail will shortly become apparent as it leads away from the west fork to continue along the steep west bank of the east fork of Hanakoa Stream. On the way the trail passes above several small pools and waterfalls where landslides may make the trail too hazardous to attempt. It finally reaches the large pool below Hanakoa Falls.

Cool refreshing water from the rain forest 3000 feet above cascades into the pool. Beware of rocks coming down with the water. A second waterfall to the east cascades only during wet weather. A swim is

Hanakoa Falls

especially enjoyable after a long hike down the Kalalau Trail. The deep, wide pool is surrounded by high cliffs on three sides. These cliffs seem to be a favorite haunt of the white-tailed tropic bird, a large swallow-like bird with the peculiar habit of flying full speed toward cliffs and veering to safety inches before impact.

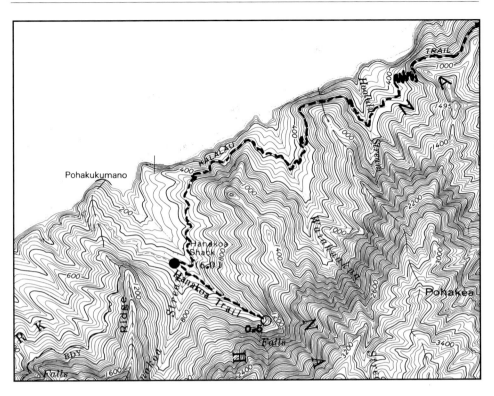

To lie in the warm sun after a long hike and a cool swim, looking up at these graceful white birds playing near the waterfall and cliffs, is one of life's better pastimes.

I am a part of all that
*   I have met;*
Yet all experience is
*   an arch wherethro'*
Gleams that untravell'd world,
*   whose margin fades*
For ever and for ever
*   when I move.*

— Alfred, Lord Tennyson
Ulysses

Ancient Lava Tube and Seashore

Index

Selected Readings

Carlquist, Sherwin. 1980. *Hawaii: A Natural History*. 2nd ed. Pacific Tropical Botanical Gardens, Lawai, HI.

Chisholm, Craig. 1992. *Hawaiian Hiking Trails*. The Fernglen Press, Lake Oswego, OR.

Clare, John R. K. 1990. *Beaches of Kaua'i and Ni'ihau*. University of Hawaii Press, Honolulu, HI.

Cuddihy, Linda W. and Stone, Charles P. 1990. *Alteration of Native Hawaiian Vegetation*. University of Hawaii Press, Hoholulu, HI.

Daws, Gaven. 1988. *Hawaii, The Islands of Life*. The Nature Conservancy of Hawaii. Signature Publishing, Honolulu, HI.

Degener, O. 1975. *Plants of Hawaii National Park*. Reprint. Braun-Brumfield, Ann Arbor, Michigan.

Hawaii Audubon Society. 1984. *Hawaii's Birds*. Honolulu, HI.

Kepel, Angela Kay. 1983. *Hawaiian Heritage Plants*. The Oriental Publishing Company, Honolulu, HI.

Merlin, Mark P. 1980. *Hawaiian Coastal Plants*. The Oriental Publishing Company, Honolulu, HI.

Neal, M. C. 1965. *In Gardens of Hawaii*. Rev. ed. B.P. Bishop Museum Special Publication 50, Honolulu, HI.

Pukui, Mary K. 1974. *Place Names of Hawaii*. 2nd ed. University of Hawaii Press, Honolulu, HI.

Rock, J. F. 1974. *The Indigenous Trees of the Hawaiian Islands*. Reprint of 1913 edition. Charles E. Tuttle, Rutland, VT.

Sohmer, S. H. & R. Gustafson. 1987. *Plants and Flowers of Hawai'i*. University of Hawaii Press, Honolulu, HI.

Sterns, Harold T. 1985. *Geology of the State of Hawaii*. Pacific Books, Palo Alto, California.

Stone, Charles P. and Stone, Danielle B. 1989. *Conservation Biology in Hawai'i*. University of Hawaii Press, Honolulu, HI.

University of Hawaii, Department of Geography. 1983. *Atlas of Hawaii*. The University Press of Hawaii, Honolulu, HI.

Order Form

The Fernglen Press
473 Sixth Street, Suite K
Lake Oswego, Oregon 97034, USA
Telephone (503) 635-4719

QUANTITY   AMOUNT

Please, send me the following books by Craig Chisholm:

_____   *Hawaiian Hiking Trails*, $14.95   _____
                      (covering all the islands)
_____   *Kauai Hiking Trails*, $12.95   _____
_____   *Hawaii, the Big Island, Hiking Trails*, $12.95   _____
_____   *Oahu Hiking Trails*, $12.95 (publ. 1992)   _____

Also use this form to order the campanion travel guides:

_____   *Maui, a Paradise Guide*, $9.95   _____
                      by Greg and Christie Stilson
_____   *Kauai, a Paradise Guide*, $9.95   _____
                      by Don and Bea Donohugh
_____   *Oahu, a Paradise Guide*, $9.95   _____
                      by Ken Bierly
_____   *Hawaii the Big Island, a Paradise Guide*, $9.95 _____
                      by John Penisten

For the young traveller, a fun educational activity book:

_____   *My Travels in Hawaii*, $3.95   _____
                      by Paul and Steve Roth

                                                    Total for books   _____

                        Shipping: First book $2.00   _____
                                        Each additional book .50   _____
                                        Air Mail each book $4.00   _____

                        AMOUNT ENCLOSED (U.S. funds)   _____

I understand that I may return any book for a full refund if not satisfied.

Name: _____

Address: _____

City: _____ State: _____ Zip: _____